Homestyle Casseroles

FAVORITE
BrandName
RECIPES™

pil
Publications International, Ltd.

Pictured on the front cover *(clockwise from top left):* Manicotti *(page 87),* Beef in Wine Sauce *(page 82),* Biscuit-Topped Chicken Pot Pie *(page 140)* and Hearty Shepherd's Pie *(page 54).*

Pictured on the back cover *(left to right):* Artichoke-Olive Chicken Bake *(page 122),* Egg & Sausage Casserole *(page 42)* and Apple & Carrot Casserole *(page 258).*

ISBN-13: 978-1-4508-4652-3
ISBN-10: 1-4508-4652-1

Library of Congress Control Number: 2012930243

Manufactured in China.

8 7 6 5 4 3 2 1

Microwave Cooking: Microwave ovens vary in wattage. Use the cooking times as guidelines and check for doneness before adding more time.

Preparation/Cooking Times: Preparation times are based on the approximate amount of time required to assemble the recipe before cooking, baking, chilling or serving. These times include preparation steps such as measuring, chopping and mixing. The fact that some preparations and cooking can be done simultaneously is taken into account. Preparation of optional ingredients and serving suggestions is not included.

Publications International, Ltd.

Table of Contents

Oven-Ready Breakfasts

Feta Brunch Bake

  1 medium red bell pepper
  2 bags (10 ounces each) fresh spinach, stemmed
  6 eggs
  1½ cups (6 ounces) crumbled feta cheese
  ⅓ cup chopped onion
  2 tablespoons chopped fresh parsley
  ¼ teaspoon dried dill weed
     Dash black pepper

1. Preheat broiler. Place bell pepper on foil-lined broiler pan. Broil, 4 inches from heat, 15 to 20 minutes or until blackened on all sides, turning every 5 minutes with tongs. Place in paper bag; close bag and set aside to cool 15 to 20 minutes. Cut around core, twist and remove. Cut bell pepper in half and rub off skin; rinse under cold water. Cut into ½-inch pieces.

2. Fill medium saucepan half full with water; bring to a boil over high heat. Add spinach. Return to a boil; boil 2 to 3 minutes or until wilted. Drain; immediately plunge spinach into medium bowl of cold water. Drain; let stand until cool enough to handle. Squeeze spinach to remove excess water; finely chop.

3. Preheat oven to 400°F. Grease 1-quart baking dish.

4. Beat eggs in large bowl with electric mixer at medium speed until foamy. Stir in bell pepper, spinach, cheese, onion, parsley, dill weed and black pepper. Pour egg mixture into prepared dish.

5. Bake 20 minutes or until set. Let stand 5 minutes before serving.

Makes 4 servings

Cheddar Apple Breakfast Lasagna

1 cup sour cream
⅓ cup brown sugar
2 packages (9 ounces each) frozen French toast
½ pound sliced ham
2 cups (8 ounces) SARGENTO® ARTISAN BLENDS™
  Shredded Double Cheddar Cheese, divided
1 can (20 ounces) apple pie filling
1 cup granola with raisins

1. Blend sour cream and brown sugar in small bowl; chill until serving time.

2. Place 6 French toast slices in greased 13×9-inch baking pan. Layer ham, 1½ cups cheese and remaining 6 slices of French toast in pan. Spread with apple filling; sprinkle with granola.

3. Bake in preheated 350°F oven 25 minutes. Top with remaining cheese; bake 5 minutes more or until cheese is melted and casserole is hot. Serve with sour cream mixture.   Makes 6 servings

Prep Time: 20 minutes
Bake Time: 30 minutes

Overnight Ham and Cheese Strata

12 slices white bread, crust removed
 1 (10-ounce) package frozen chopped broccoli, thawed and drained
 2 (5-ounce) cans HORMEL® chunk ham, drained and flaked
 6 eggs, beaten
 2 cups milk
¼ cup minced onion
¼ teaspoon dry mustard
 3 cups shredded Cheddar cheese

Cut bread into small cubes. Layer one-half of bread cubes, broccoli and chunk ham in buttered 13×9-inch baking dish. Top with remaining bread cubes. Beat together eggs, milk, onion and dry mustard. Pour over bread. Sprinkle with cheese. Cover and refrigerate overnight. Heat oven to 325°F. Bake 55 to 60 minutes or until eggs are set.   Makes 12 servings

Cornmeal, Sausage and Chile Casserole

4 ounces turkey breakfast sausage links, removed from casings
½ cup diced onion
1 medium red bell pepper, diced
1 teaspoon ground cumin
½ to 1 teaspoon chili powder
1 cup chicken broth
½ cup yellow cornmeal
3 egg whites
1 can (about 4 ounces) diced mild green chiles, drained
½ cup (2 ounces) shredded Cheddar cheese
3 eggs, beaten
¾ cup salsa

1. Heat large nonstick skillet over medium-high heat. Add sausage, onion and bell pepper; cook 5 minutes or until sausage is browned and vegetables are crisp-tender, stirring to break up meat. Add cumin and chili powder; cook and stir 1 minute.

2. Add broth to skillet; bring to a boil. Gradually add cornmeal; cook 1 minute, stirring constantly. Transfer mixture to large bowl; set aside to cool slightly.

3. Preheat oven to 375°F. Spray 11×7-inch baking dish with nonstick cooking spray.

4. Beat egg whites in small bowl with electric mixer at high speed until stiff peaks form. Stir chiles and cheese into cornmeal mixture. Stir in whole eggs. Gently fold beaten egg whites into cornmeal mixture. Spoon mixture into prepared dish.

5. Bake 30 minutes or until center is set and edges are lightly browned. Cool slightly. Serve with salsa.
Makes 6 servings

Cornmeal, Sausage and Chile Casserole

Make-Ahead Breakfast Casserole

2½ cups seasoned croutons

1 pound **BOB EVANS®** Original Recipe Roll Sausage

2¼ cups milk

4 eggs

1 (10½-ounce) can condensed cream of mushroom soup, undiluted

1 (10-ounce) package frozen chopped spinach, thawed and squeezed dry

1 (4-ounce) can mushrooms, drained and chopped

1 cup (4 ounces) shredded sharp Cheddar cheese

1 cup (4 ounces) shredded Monterey Jack cheese

¼ teaspoon dry mustard

Fresh herb sprigs and carrot strips (optional)

Picante sauce or salsa (optional)

Spread croutons on bottom of greased 13×9-inch baking dish. Crumble sausage into medium skillet. Cook over medium heat until browned, stirring occasionally. Drain off any drippings. Spread over croutons. Whisk milk and eggs in large bowl until blended. Stir in soup, spinach, mushrooms, cheeses and mustard. Pour egg mixture over sausage and croutons. Refrigerate overnight. Preheat oven to 325°F. Bake egg mixture 50 to 55 minutes or until set and lightly browned on top. Garnish with herb sprigs and carrot strips, if desired. Serve hot with picante sauce, if desired. Refrigerate leftovers.   Makes 10 to 12 servings

Mushroom and Arugula Quiche

   1 tablespoon olive oil
  ½ cup chopped onion
   2 cloves garlic, minced
1½ cups sliced mushrooms (5 to 6 ounces)
   1 package (5 ounces) DOLE® Baby Arugula with Baby Spinach Blend
   1 cup (4 ounces) shredded Swiss cheese
  ¼ cup grated Parmesan cheese, divided
   1 (9-inch) frozen deep-dish pie shell, thawed
   4 eggs, well beaten
  ½ cup half-and-half
  ¼ teaspoon salt
     Pinch ground black pepper
     Pinch ground nutmeg

• Preheat oven to 375°F.

• Heat oil in large nonstick skillet over medium-high heat. Add onion and garlic; cook, stirring often, until tender, 3 to 4 minutes. Add mushrooms; cook, stirring occasionally, until excess moisture has evaporated and starts to brown, 4 to 5 minutes. Add the salad blend and cook, stirring until wilted and almost dry, 3 to 4 minutes. Remove from heat; cool slightly.

• Mix together cooled vegetables and Swiss cheese. Sprinkle ½ Parmesan cheese on bottom of pie shell. Top with vegetable mixture.

• Stir together eggs, half-and-half, salt and spices; pour into the pie shell. Sprinkle with remaining Parmesan cheese. Bake 30 minutes or until knife inserted near center comes out clean.   Makes 4 to 6 servings

Prep Time: 15 minutes
Bake Time: 30 minutes

Aunt Marilyn's Cinnamon French Toast Casserole

1 large loaf French bread, cut into 1½-inch slices
3½ cups milk
9 eggs
1½ cups granulated sugar, divided
1 tablespoon vanilla
½ teaspoon salt
6 to 8 baking apples, such as McIntosh or Cortland, peeled and sliced
1 teaspoon ground cinnamon
½ teaspoon ground nutmeg
Powdered sugar (optional)

1. Grease 13×9-inch baking dish or casserole. Arrange bread slices in single layer in prepared dish.

2. Whisk milk, eggs, 1 cup granulated sugar, vanilla and salt in large bowl until well blended. Pour half of mixture over bread. Layer apple slices over bread. Pour remaining half of egg mixture over apples.

3. Combine remaining ½ cup granulated sugar, cinnamon and nutmeg in small bowl; sprinkle over casserole. Cover and refrigerate overnight.

4. Preheat oven to 350°F. Bake, uncovered, 1 hour or until set. Sprinkle with powdered sugar, if desired.   Makes 6 to 8 servings

Biscuit and Sausage Bake

2 cups biscuit baking mix
½ cup milk
1 egg
1 teaspoon vanilla
1 cup fresh or frozen blueberries
6 fully cooked breakfast sausage links, thawed if frozen
   Maple syrup

1. Preheat oven to 350°F. Coat 8-inch square baking pan with nonstick cooking spray.

2. Whisk baking mix, milk, egg and vanilla in medium bowl. Gently fold in blueberries. (Batter will be stiff.) Spread batter in prepared pan. Cut each sausage link into small pieces; sprinkle over batter.

3. Bake 22 minutes or until top is lightly browned. Serve with maple syrup.

Makes 6 servings

Ham 'n' Apple Breakfast Casserole

1 package (15 ounces) refrigerated pie crusts (2 crusts)
1 pound thinly sliced ham, cut into bite-size pieces
1 can (about 21 ounces) apple pie filling
1 cup (4 ounces) shredded sharp Cheddar cheese
¼ cup plus 1 teaspoon sugar, divided
½ teaspoon ground cinnamon

1. Preheat oven to 425°F.

2. Place one crust in 9-inch pie pan, allowing edges to hang over sides. Arrange half of ham pieces in bottom; spoon apple pie filling over ham. Arrange remaining ham on top of apples; sprinkle with cheese.

3. Mix ¼ cup sugar and cinnamon in small bowl; sprinkle evenly over cheese. Arrange second crust over filling and crimp edges together. Brush crust lightly with water and sprinkle with remaining 1 teaspoon sugar. Cut slits for steam to escape.

4. Bake 20 to 25 minutes or until crust is golden brown. Cool 15 minutes before serving.

Makes 6 servings

Breakfast Casserole

6 large eggs, beaten
½ cup sour cream
1 can (15 ounces) VEG•ALL® Original Mixed Vegetables, drained
1 cup frozen cubed hash brown potatoes, thawed
1 cup smoked sausage links, chopped
1 cup shredded pepper-jack cheese
2 tablespoons canned jalapeño pepper slices
1 cup broken tortilla chips

Preheat oven to 350°F.

In medium bowl, combine eggs and sour cream until smooth. Fold in remaining ingredients except tortilla chips.

Transfer mixture to greased 11×7-inch baking dish. Bake for 25 to 30 minutes or until eggs are set and puffed.

Top with tortilla chips and bake an additional 5 minutes. Serve with additional sour cream on the side, if desired.

Serve with fresh fruit for breakfast.   Makes 6 to 8 servings

tip For a milder flavor, substitute chopped fresh cilantro for the sliced jalapeño peppers.

Breakfast Casserole

Crustless Ham & Spinach Tart

6 tablespoons shredded Parmesan cheese, divided

1 teaspoon olive oil

1 cup finely chopped onion

2 cloves garlic, minced

1 package (10 ounces) frozen chopped spinach, thawed and squeezed dry

3 slices deli ham, cut into strips (3 ounces total)

1¼ cups milk

3 eggs

1½ tablespoons all-purpose flour

1 tablespoon minced fresh basil *or* 2 teaspoons dried basil

½ teaspoon black pepper

⅛ teaspoon ground nutmeg

1. Preheat oven to 350°F. Lightly spray 9-inch glass pie plate with nonstick cooking spray. Sprinkle with 2 tablespoons cheese.

2. Heat oil in medium nonstick skillet over medium-high heat. Add onion; cook and stir 2 minutes or until soft. Add garlic; cook 1 minute. Stir in spinach and ham, mixing well. Spread mixture evenly in prepared pie plate.

3. Combine milk, eggs, flour, basil, pepper and nutmeg in medium bowl; pour over spinach mixture.

4. Bake 50 minutes or until knife inserted into center comes out clean. Sprinkle with remaining 4 tablespoons cheese.

Makes 6 servings

Hash Brown Casserole

2 cups (8 ounces) shredded cheddar cheese
3 cartons (4 ounces *each*) cholesterol-free egg product or 6 large eggs, well beaten
1 can (12 fluid ounces) NESTLÉ® CARNATION® Evaporated Fat Free Milk
1 teaspoon salt (optional)
½ teaspoon ground black pepper
1 package (30 ounces) frozen shredded hash brown potatoes
1 medium onion, chopped
1 small green bell pepper, chopped
1 cup diced ham or 10 slices turkey bacon, cooked and chopped

PREHEAT oven to 350°F. Grease 13×9-inch baking dish.

COMBINE cheese, egg product, evaporated milk, salt and black pepper in large bowl. Add potatoes, onion, bell pepper and ham; mix well. Pour mixture into prepared baking dish.

BAKE for 60 to 65 minutes or until set.   Makes 12 servings

Prep Time: 15 minutes
Baking Time: 60 minutes

Sunrise Squares

1 pound BOB EVANS® Original Recipe Roll Sausage
2 slices bread, cut into ½-inch cubes (about 2 cups)
1 cup (4 ounces) shredded sharp Cheddar cheese
6 eggs
2 cups milk
½ teaspoon salt
½ teaspoon dry mustard

Preheat oven to 350°F. Crumble sausage into medium skillet. Cook over medium heat until browned, stirring occasionally. Drain off any drippings. Spread bread cubes in greased 11×7-inch baking dish; top with sausage and cheese. Whisk eggs, milk, salt and mustard until well blended; pour over cheese. Bake 30 to 40 minutes or until set. Let stand 5 minutes before cutting into squares; serve hot. Refrigerate leftovers.

Makes 6 servings

Serving Suggestion: Serve these squares between toasted English muffins.

Hash Brown Casserole

Bacon and Maple Grits Puff

8 slices bacon
2 cups milk
1¼ cups water
1 cup quick-cooking grits
½ teaspoon salt
½ cup maple syrup
4 eggs
Minced fresh chives (optional)

1. Preheat oven to 350°F. Grease 1½-quart soufflé dish or round casserole.

2. Cook bacon in large skillet over medium-high heat until crisp. Drain on paper towels; set aside. Reserve 2 tablespoons bacon fat.

3. Combine milk, water, grits and salt in medium saucepan; bring to a boil over medium heat, stirring frequently. Reduce heat to low; simmer 2 minutes or until mixture thickens, stirring constantly. Remove from heat; stir in maple syrup and reserved 2 tablespoons bacon fat.

4. Crumble bacon; reserve ¼ cup for garnish. Stir remaining crumbled bacon into grits mixture.

5. Beat eggs in medium bowl with electric mixer at high speed until thick and pale yellow. Stir spoonful of grits mixture into eggs until well blended. Fold egg mixture into remaining grits mixture until blended. Spoon into prepared dish.

6. Bake 1 hour and 20 minutes or until knife inserted into center comes out clean. Top with reserved ¼ cup bacon and chives, if desired. Serve immediately.

Makes 6 to 8 servings

Note: Puff will fall slightly after being removed from oven.

Spicy Sausage Popover Pizza

½ **pound turkey breakfast sausage patties, crumbled**
½ **pound ground turkey**
⅓ **cup chopped onion**
1 **clove garlic, minced**
¾ **cup chopped red bell pepper**
1½ **cups all-purpose flour**
¼ **teaspoon salt**
¼ **teaspoon red pepper flakes**
1 **cup milk**
3 **eggs**
1 **cup (4 ounces) shredded Cheddar cheese**
½ **cup (2 ounces) shredded mozzarella cheese**
½ **cup pizza sauce**

1. Preheat oven to 425°F. Spray 13×9-inch baking dish with nonstick cooking spray.

2. Heat large nonstick skillet over medium heat. Add sausage, ground turkey, onion and garlic; cook until meat is browned, stirring to break up meat. Drain fat. Stir in bell pepper.

3. Combine flour, salt and red pepper flakes in medium bowl. Combine milk and eggs in another medium bowl; whisk into flour mixture until smooth. Pour into prepared baking dish. Sprinkle sausage mixture over top. Sprinkle with cheeses.

4. Bake 21 to 23 minutes or until puffed and golden brown. Cut into wedges.

5. Meanwhile, microwave pizza sauce on HIGH 1 minute. Top each wedge evenly with pizza sauce.

Makes 8 servings

Brunch Casserole

1 pound mild bulk pork sausage
3 cups frozen hash brown potatoes, thawed
1 large green bell pepper, diced
1 can (11 ounces) nacho cheese soup
¼ cup milk
1 cup (4 ounces) shredded Cheddar cheese

1. Preheat oven to 350°F. Grease 11×7-inch casserole.

2. Brown sausage in large skillet over medium heat 6 to 8 minutes, stirring to break up meat. Drain fat. Combine potatoes, bell pepper and two thirds of soup in medium bowl. Spoon into prepared casserole. Layer sausage over potato mixture. Stir remaining soup and milk in small bowl. Spoon over sausage. Sprinkle with cheese.

3. Bake 20 minutes or until cheese is melted and sauce is bubbly.

Makes 4 to 6 servings

Apple & Raisin Oven Pancake

1 large baking apple, cored and thinly sliced
⅓ cup golden raisins
2 tablespoons packed brown sugar
½ teaspoon ground cinnamon
4 eggs
⅔ cup milk
⅔ cup all-purpose flour
2 tablespoons butter, melted
     Powdered sugar (optional)

1. Preheat oven to 350°F. Spray 9-inch pie plate with nonstick cooking spray. Combine apple, raisins, brown sugar and cinnamon in medium bowl. Transfer to prepared pie plate.

2. Bake 10 to 15 minutes or until apple begins to soften. Remove from oven. *Increase oven temperature to 450°F.*

3. Meanwhile, whisk eggs, milk, flour and butter in medium bowl until blended. Pour batter over apple mixture.

4. Bake 15 minutes or until pancake is golden brown. Sprinkle with powdered sugar, if desired.

Makes 6 servings

Delicious Ham & Cheese Puff Pie

2 cups (about 1 pound) diced cooked ham
1 package (10 ounces) frozen chopped spinach, thawed and squeezed dry
½ cup diced red bell pepper
4 green onions, sliced
3 eggs
¾ cup *each* all-purpose flour, shredded Swiss cheese and milk
1 tablespoon prepared mustard
1 teaspoon *each* grated lemon peel and dried dill weed
½ teaspoon *each* garlic salt and black pepper

1. Preheat oven to 425°F. Grease 2-quart round casserole.

2. Combine ham, spinach, bell pepper and green onions in prepared casserole. Beat eggs in medium bowl. Stir in flour, cheese, milk, mustard, lemon peel, dill weed, garlic salt and black pepper; pour over ham mixture.

3. Bake 30 to 35 minutes or until puffed and browned.　　Makes 4 to 6 servings

Oven Breakfast Hash

2 pounds baking potatoes, unpeeled (5 or 6 medium)
1 pound BOB EVANS® Original Recipe Roll Sausage
1 (12-ounce can) evaporated milk
⅓ cup chopped green onions
1 tablespoon Worcestershire sauce
½ teaspoon salt
¼ teaspoon black pepper
¼ cup dried bread crumbs
1 tablespoon melted butter or margarine
½ teaspoon paprika

Cook potatoes in boiling water until fork-tender. Drain and coarsely chop or mash. Preheat oven to 350°F. Crumble and cook sausage in medium skillet until browned. Drain and transfer to large bowl. Stir in potatoes, milk, green onions, Worcestershire sauce, salt and pepper. Pour into greased 2½- or 3-quart casserole dish. Sprinkle with bread crumbs; drizzle with melted butter. Sprinkle with paprika. Bake, uncovered, 30 to 35 minutes or until casserole bubbles and top is browned. Refrigerate leftovers.　　Makes 6 to 8 servings

French Toast Strata

4 cups (4 ounces) day-old French or Italian bread, cut into large cubes

⅓ cup golden raisins

3 ounces cream cheese, cut into ¼-inch cubes

3 eggs

1½ cups milk

½ cup maple syrup, plus additional for serving

1 teaspoon vanilla

2 tablespoons sugar

1 teaspoon ground cinnamon

1. Spray 11×7-inch baking dish with nonstick cooking spray. Place bread cubes in even layer in prepared dish; sprinkle raisins and cream cheese evenly over bread.

2. Beat eggs in medium bowl with electric mixer at medium speed until blended. Add milk, ½ cup maple syrup and vanilla; mix well. Pour egg mixture evenly over bread mixture. Cover; refrigerate at least 4 hours or overnight.

3. Preheat oven to 350°F.

4. Combine sugar and cinnamon in small bowl; sprinkle evenly over strata.

5. Bake 40 to 45 minutes or until puffed, golden brown and knife inserted into center comes out clean. Serve with additional maple syrup. Makes 6 servings

Serving Suggestion: Serve with mixed fresh fruit.

Breakfast Bake

1 pound ground pork sausage

1 teaspoon Italian seasoning

½ teaspoon salt

6 eggs

2 cups milk

½ cup **CREAM OF WHEAT®** Hot Cereal (Instant, 1-minute, 2½-minute or 10-minute cook time), uncooked

1 teaspoon **TRAPPEY'S®** Red Devil™ Cayenne Pepper Sauce

4 cups cubed bread stuffing (potato bread recommended)

2 cups Cheddar cheese, shredded

1. Brown sausage in skillet, pressing with fork or spatula to crumble as it cooks. Sprinkle on Italian seasoning and salt; set aside.

2. Combine eggs, milk, Cream of Wheat and pepper sauce in large mixing bowl; mix well. Add cooked sausage and bread stuffing; toss to combine. Pour mixture into 13×9-inch casserole pan; cover. Refrigerate at least 4 hours or overnight.

3. Preheat oven to 350°F. Remove cover and sprinkle cheese over casserole. Cover pan with aluminum foil; bake 30 minutes. Remove foil; bake 15 minutes longer. Serve warm.   Makes 8 servings

Prep Time: 30 minutes

Start to Finish Time: 4 to 12 hours soaking, 45 minutes baking

Serving Suggestion: Serve this dish with a salad and some fresh fruit on holiday mornings or for a special breakfast.

Ham & Cheese Grits Soufflé

3 cups water
¾ cup quick-cooking grits
½ teaspoon salt
½ cup (2 ounces) shredded mozzarella cheese
2 ounces ham, finely chopped
2 tablespoons minced fresh chives
2 eggs, separated
Dash hot pepper sauce

1. Preheat oven to 375°F. Grease 1½-quart soufflé dish or deep round casserole.

2. Bring water to a boil in medium saucepan; stir in grits and salt. Cook and stir 5 minutes or until thickened. Stir in cheese, ham, chives, egg yolks and hot pepper sauce.

3. Beat egg whites in small bowl with electric mixer at high speed until stiff peaks form; fold into grits mixture. Spoon into prepared dish.

4. Bake 30 minutes or until puffed and golden. Serve immediately.

Makes 4 to 6 servings

Spinach Pie

1 tablespoon olive oil
1 pound fresh spinach, washed, drained and stems removed
1 medium potato, cooked and mashed
2 eggs, beaten
½ cup BELGIOIOSO® Ricotta con Latte Cheese
¼ cup grated BELGIOIOSO® Romano Cheese
Salt to taste

Preheat oven to 350°F. Grease 8-inch round cake pan with olive oil. Tear spinach into bite-sized pieces. Combine spinach, potato, eggs, BelGioioso Ricotta con Latte Cheese, BelGioioso Romano Cheese and salt in large bowl. Spoon mixture into prepared pan. Bake 15 to 20 minutes or until set. Season to taste with salt.

Makes 6 servings

Ham & Cheese Grits Soufflé

Cheddar and Leek Strata

8 eggs, lightly beaten

2 cups milk

½ cup porter ale or beer

2 cloves garlic, minced

Salt and black pepper

1 loaf (16 ounces) sourdough bread, cut into ½-inch cubes

2 small leeks, coarsely chopped

1 red bell pepper, chopped

1½ cups (6 ounces) shredded Swiss cheese

1½ cups (6 ounces) shredded sharp Cheddar cheese

1. Grease 13×9-inch baking dish. Combine eggs, milk, ale, garlic, salt and black pepper in large bowl. Beat until well blended.

2. Place half of bread cubes on bottom of prepared dish. Sprinkle half of leeks and half of bell pepper over bread cubes. Top with ¾ cup Swiss cheese and ¾ cup Cheddar cheese. Repeat layers. Pour egg mixture evenly over top.

3. Cover tightly with plastic wrap or foil. Weigh top of strata down with slightly smaller baking dish. Refrigerate 2 hours or overnight.

4. Preheat oven to 350°F. Bake, uncovered, 40 to 45 minutes or until center is set. Serve immediately.

Makes 12 servings

Chorizo and Cheddar Breakfast Casserole

8 ounces chorizo sausage, removed from casing

1 cup diced onion

1 medium green bell pepper, chopped

1 jalapeño pepper,* chopped

6 eggs, beaten

¾ cup biscuit baking mix

⅔ cup buttermilk**

Salt and black pepper

1 cup (4 ounces) shredded Cheddar cheese

¼ cup chopped fresh cilantro

½ cup sour cream (optional)

Chopped tomato (optional)

Jalapeño peppers can sting and irritate the skin, so wear rubber gloves when handling peppers and do not touch your eyes.

**If you don't have buttermilk, substitute 2 teaspoons vinegar or lemon juice plus enough milk to equal ⅔ cup. Let stand 5 minutes.*

1. Preheat oven to 350°F. Coat 11×7-inch baking pan with nonstick cooking spray.

2. Heat large nonstick skillet over medium heat. Add chorizo; cook 4 minutes or until browned, stirring to break up meat. Drain fat. Add onion, bell pepper and jalapeño pepper; cook and stir 6 minutes or until crisp-tender. Transfer to prepared pan.

3. Combine eggs, baking mix, buttermilk, salt and black pepper in medium bowl; mix well. Pour over chorizo mixture.

4. Bake 30 minutes or until knife inserted into center comes out clean. Sprinkle evenly with cheese and cilantro. Let stand 10 minutes. Serve with sour cream and tomato, if desired.

Makes 6 servings

Chorizo and Cheddar Breakfast Casserole

Oven-Baked French Toast

12 slices cinnamon bread or cinnamon raisin bread
1 pint (16 ounces) half-and-half or light cream
2 eggs
6 tablespoons I CAN'T BELIEVE IT'S NOT BUTTER!® Spread, melted
2 tablespoons firmly packed brown sugar
2 teaspoons vanilla extract
1 teaspoon grated orange peel (optional)
¼ teaspoon ground cinnamon
⅛ teaspoon ground nutmeg (optional)

Preheat oven to 350°F.

In lightly greased 13×9-inch baking pan, arrange bread slices in two layers.

In large bowl, with wire whisk, blend remaining ingredients. Evenly pour over bread slices, pressing bread down until some liquid is absorbed and bread does not float.

Bake 45 minutes or until center reaches 160°F. and bread is golden brown. Serve hot and sprinkle, if desired, with confectioners' sugar.   Makes 6 servings

Hash Brown Casserole with Bacon

1 package (32 ounces) frozen Southern-style hash brown potatoes, thawed
1 container (16 ounces) sour cream
1 can (10¾ ounces) condensed cream of chicken soup, undiluted
1½ cups (6 ounces) shredded sharp Cheddar cheese
¾ cup thinly sliced green onions
4 slices bacon, crisp-cooked and crumbled
2 teaspoons hot pepper sauce
¼ teaspoon garlic salt

1. Preheat oven to 350°F. Spray 13×9-inch baking pan with nonstick cooking spray.

2. Combine potatoes, sour cream, soup, cheese, green onions, bacon, hot pepper sauce and garlic salt in large bowl. Spoon into prepared pan.

3. Bake 55 to 60 minutes or until potatoes are tender and cooked through. Stir before serving.   Makes 12 servings

Hearty Breakfast Custard Casserole

1 pound (2 medium-large) Colorado baking potatoes
   Salt and black pepper
8 ounces low-fat bulk pork sausage, cooked and crumbled *or* 6 ounces finely diced
   lean ham *or* 6 ounces turkey bacon, cooked and crumbled
⅓ cup julienne-sliced roasted red pepper *or* 1 jar (2 ounces) sliced pimientos, drained
1 cup low-fat milk
3 eggs
3 tablespoons chopped fresh chives or green onion tops *or* ¾ teaspoon dried thyme
   or oregano leaves
   Salsa and low-fat sour cream or plain yogurt (optional)

Heat oven to 375°F. Grease 8- or 9-inch square baking dish or other small casserole. Peel potatoes and slice very thinly; arrange half of potatoes in baking dish. Sprinkle with salt and black pepper. Cover with half of sausage. Arrange remaining potatoes on top; sprinkle with salt and black pepper. Top with remaining sausage and roasted red pepper. Beat milk, eggs and chives until blended. Pour over potatoes. Cover baking dish with foil and bake 35 to 45 minutes or until potatoes are tender. Uncover and bake 5 to 10 minutes more. Serve with salsa and sour cream, if desired.

Makes 4 to 5 servings

Favorite recipe from **Colorado Potato Administrative Committee**

tip

Casserole can refer both to a specific baking dish and the food it contains. A casserole dish is a deep round or oval ovenproof container often with two short handles. It may or may not be covered. They are made of glass, earthenware or porcelain and are measured by their volumes in quarts.

Bacon and Eggs Brunch Casserole

1 tube (8 ounces) refrigerated crescent roll dough
6 eggs
½ cup milk
1 cup (4 ounces) SARGENTO® Chef Style Shredded Mild Cheddar Cheese
8 slices bacon, diced and cooked crisp

1. Spray a 13×9-inch baking pan with non-stick cooking spray. Unroll dough and press into bottom of pan. Bake in preheated 350°F oven 10 minutes.

2. Beat together eggs and milk in medium bowl. Pour over partially baked dough. Sprinkle with cheese and bacon; return to oven and bake 25 minutes more or until center is set.
Makes 6 servings

Prep Time: 15 minutes
Bake Time: 35 minutes

Oven French Toast

Butter
3 eggs, well beaten
¾ cup milk
1 tablespoon sugar
1½ teaspoons WATKINS® Clear Vanilla Extract
⅛ teaspoon WATKINS® Nutmeg
8 slices day-old French or white bread
½ teaspoon WATKINS® Ground Cinnamon mixed with 2 tablespoons sugar (optional)
Pancake syrup (optional)

Preheat oven to 500°F. Generously grease 15×10×1-inch pan with butter. Beat eggs, milk, sugar, vanilla and nutmeg in shallow bowl until well blended. Heat pan in oven for 1 minute; remove from oven. Dip bread slices, one at a time, into egg mixture. Arrange on hot pan. Drizzle any remaining egg mixture over bread.

Bake for 7 to 10 minutes or until bottoms of bread slices are golden brown. Turn bread, bake for 3 to 5 minutes longer or until golden brown. Sprinkle with cinnamon-sugar or serve with syrup, if desired.
Makes 4 servings

Bacon and Eggs Brunch Casserole

Egg & Sausage Casserole

8 ounces bulk pork sausage

3 tablespoons butter, divided

2 tablespoons all-purpose flour

Salt and black pepper

1¼ cups milk

2 cups frozen hash brown potatoes, thawed

4 eggs, hard-cooked and sliced

½ cup cornflake crumbs

¼ cup sliced green onions

1. Preheat oven to 350°F. Spray 2-quart oval baking dish with nonstick cooking spray.

2. Brown sausage in large skillet over medium-high heat 6 to 8 minutes, stirring to break up meat. Drain fat. Transfer to plate.

3. Melt 2 tablespoons butter in same skillet over medium heat. Stir in flour, salt and pepper until smooth. Gradually stir in milk; cook and stir until thickened. Add sausage, potatoes and eggs; stir until blended. Transfer to prepared baking dish.

4. Melt remaining 1 tablespoon butter in small saucepan over low heat. Add cornflake crumbs; stir until combined. Sprinkle evenly over casserole.

5. Bake 30 minutes or until hot and bubbly. Sprinkle with green onions just before serving.
Makes 6 servings

Spinach Cheese Strata

6 slices whole wheat bread
2 tablespoons butter, softened
1 cup (4 ounces) shredded Cheddar cheese
½ cup (2 ounces) shredded Monterey Jack cheese
1¼ cups milk
6 eggs, lightly beaten
1 package (10 ounces) frozen chopped spinach, thawed and squeezed dry
Salt and black pepper

1. Grease 13×9-inch baking dish. Spread bread with butter; arrange in single layer in prepared dish. Sprinkle with cheeses.

2. Combine milk, eggs, spinach, salt and pepper in large bowl; stir well. Pour over bread and cheese. Cover; refrigerate at least 6 hours or overnight.

3. Preheat oven to 350°F. Bake, uncovered, about 1 hour or until puffed and golden.

Makes 4 to 6 servings

tip Any leftover strata may be stored, well covered, in the refrigerator up to 3 days. Reheat in a 300°F oven for 10 to 15 minutes or until heated through.

Spinach Cheese Strata

Sourdough and Roasted Red Pepper Breakfast Casserole

3 cups sourdough bread cubes
1 jar (12 ounces) roasted red pepper strips, drained
1 cup (4 ounces) shredded sharp Cheddar cheese
1 cup (4 ounces) shredded Monterey Jack cheese
1 cup cottage cheese
6 eggs
1 cup milk
¼ cup chopped fresh cilantro
¼ teaspoon black pepper

1. Lightly coat 11×7-inch baking dish with nonstick cooking spray. Place bread cubes in prepared baking dish. Arrange roasted peppers evenly over bread cubes; sprinkle with Cheddar and Monterey Jack cheeses.

2. Place cottage cheese in food processor or blender; process until smooth. Add eggs and milk; process just until blended. Pour over ingredients in baking dish. Sprinkle with cilantro and black pepper. Cover; refrigerate 4 hours or overnight.

3. Preheat oven to 375°F. Bake, uncovered, 40 minutes or until center is set and top is golden brown. Makes 8 servings

Mexican Omelet Roll-Ups
with Avocado Sauce

8 eggs

2 tablespoons milk

1 tablespoon butter

1½ cups (6 ounces) shredded Monterey Jack cheese

1 large tomato, seeded and chopped

¼ cup chopped fresh cilantro

8 corn tortillas

1½ cups salsa (optional)

2 medium avocados, chopped

¼ cup sour cream

2 tablespoons finely chopped onion

1 jalapeño or serrano pepper,* chopped

1 to 2 teaspoons lime juice

¼ teaspoon salt

¼ teaspoon minced garlic

Jalapeño peppers can sting and irritate the skin, so wear rubber gloves when handling peppers and do not touch your eyes.

1. Preheat oven to 350°F. Spray 13×9-inch baking dish with nonstick cooking spray.

2. Whisk eggs and milk in medium bowl until blended. Melt butter in large skillet over medium heat. Add egg mixture; cook and stir 5 minutes or until eggs are set but still soft. Remove from heat. Stir in cheese, tomato and cilantro.

3. Spoon about ⅓ cup egg mixture evenly down center of each tortilla. Roll up tortillas and place seam side down in prepared dish. Pour salsa evenly over tortillas, if desired.

4. Bake, covered, 20 minutes or until heated through.

5. Meanwhile, combine avocados, sour cream, onion, jalapeño pepper, lime juice, salt and garlic in food processor or blender; process until smooth. Serve roll-ups with avocado sauce.
Makes 8 servings

Hash Brown Breakfast Casserole

   3 cups refrigerated or frozen hash brown potatoes, thawed
1½ cups (6 ounces) finely chopped ham
   ¾ cup (3 ounces) shredded Cheddar cheese
   ¼ cup sliced green onions
   1 can (12 ounces) evaporated milk
   1 tablespoon all-purpose flour
   4 eggs
   ½ teaspoon black pepper

1. Lightly spray 8-inch square baking dish with nonstick cooking spray. Layer potatoes, ham, cheese and green onions in prepared dish.

2. Gradually whisk evaporated milk into flour in medium bowl. Stir in eggs and pepper; pour over potato mixture. Cover; refrigerate 4 hours or overnight.

3. Preheat oven to 350°F. Bake, uncovered, 55 to 60 minutes or until knife inserted into center comes out clean. Let stand 10 minutes before serving.

Makes 6 servings

Blueberry-Orange French Toast Casserole

   ½ cup sugar
   ½ cup milk
   2 eggs
   4 egg whites
   1 tablespoon grated orange peel
   ½ teaspoon vanilla
   6 slices whole wheat bread, cut into 1-inch pieces
   1 cup fresh blueberries

1. Preheat oven to 350°F. Coat 8-inch square baking dish with nonstick cooking spray.

2. Whisk sugar and milk in medium bowl until dissolved. Whisk in eggs, egg whites, orange peel and vanilla. Add bread and blueberries; toss to coat. Pour into prepared dish. Let stand 5 minutes.

3. Bake 40 to 45 minutes or until bread is browned and center is almost set. Let stand 5 minutes before serving.

Makes 6 servings

Hot 'n' Bubbly Beef

Beef, Bean and Pasta Casserole

2¾ cups uncooked whole wheat rigatoni pasta

1 pound ground beef

1 medium onion, diced

2 cloves garlic, minced

1 can (about 15 ounces) cannellini beans, rinsed and drained

1 can (about 14 ounces) diced tomatoes, drained

1 can (8 ounces) tomato sauce

2 teaspoons Italian seasoning

½ to ¾ teaspoon salt

¼ teaspoon black pepper

1 cup finely shredded Parmesan cheese

1 cup (4 ounces) shredded mozzarella cheese

1. Preheat oven to 350°F. Lightly spray 11×7-inch baking dish with nonstick cooking spray.

2. Cook pasta according to package directions; drain.

3. Meanwhile, brown beef, onion and garlic in large nonstick skillet over medium-high heat 6 to 8 minutes, stirring to break up meat. Drain fat. Add beans, tomatoes, tomato sauce, Italian seasoning, salt and pepper; cook 3 minutes.

4. Remove skillet from heat; stir in pasta and Parmesan cheese. Transfer mixture to prepared dish; sprinkle with mozzarella cheese.

5. Bake 20 minutes or until casserole is bubbly and cheese is melted.

Makes 6 servings

Variations: Any short-shape pasta can be used in this recipe. Red kidney beans can be used in place of the cannellini beans.

Beef Lasagna

1 pound ground beef

1 jar (32 ounces) pasta sauce

2 cups (16 ounces) cottage cheese

1 container (8 ounces) sour cream

8 uncooked lasagna noodles

1½ cups (6 ounces) shredded mozzarella cheese

½ cup grated Parmesan cheese

1 cup water

Fresh basil or thyme (optional)

1. Preheat oven to 350°F.

2. Brown beef in large skillet over medium-high heat 6 to 8 minutes, stirring to break up meat. Drain fat. Reduce heat to low. Add pasta sauce; cook until heated through, stirring occasionally. Combine cottage cheese and sour cream in medium bowl; blend well.

3. Spread 1½ cups meat sauce in bottom of 13×9-inch baking pan. Place 4 uncooked noodles over sauce. Top with half of cottage cheese mixture, ¾ cup mozzarella cheese, half remaining meat sauce and ¼ cup Parmesan cheese. Repeat layers starting with uncooked noodles. Top with remaining ¾ cup mozzarella cheese. Pour water around sides of pan.

4. Bake, covered, 1 hour. Bake, uncovered, 20 minutes or until hot and bubbly. Let stand 15 to 20 minutes before serving. Garnish with basil.

Makes 8 to 10 servings

Beef Lasagna

Hearty Shepherd's Pie

1½ pounds ground beef
2 cups FRENCH'S® French Fried Onions
1 can (10¾ ounces) condensed tomato soup
½ cup water
2 teaspoons Italian seasoning
¼ teaspoon *each* **salt and black pepper**
1 package (10 ounces) frozen mixed vegetables, thawed
3 cups hot mashed potatoes

1. Preheat oven to 375°F. Cook meat in large ovenproof skillet until browned; drain. Stir in *1 cup* French Fried Onions, soup, water, seasoning, salt and pepper.

2. Spoon vegetables over beef mixture. Top with mashed potatoes.

3. Bake 20 minutes or until hot. Sprinkle with remaining *1 cup* onions. Bake 2 minutes or until golden.   Makes 6 servings

Prep Time: 10 minutes
Bake Time: 27 minutes

Wild Rice Beefy Vegetable Casserole

1 pound lean ground beef
1 cup chopped onion
1 pound frozen broccoli, carrots & cauliflower blend, thawed and drained
1 can (10¾ ounces) cream of celery soup
1 can (8 ounces) tomato sauce
3 cups cooked wild rice
2 cups shredded mild Cheddar cheese, divided
2 teaspoons dried Italian seasoning
1 teaspoon salt
½ teaspoon black pepper

Preheat oven to 350°F. In large skillet, brown beef and onion; drain. Add vegetables, soup, tomato sauce, wild rice, 1½ cups cheese and seasonings; mix lightly. Place in 3-quart casserole; top with remaining ½ cup cheese. Cover; bake 25 to 30 minutes or until heated through. Uncover; bake 5 minutes.   Makes 6 to 8 servings

Favorite recipe from **Minnesota Cultivated Wild Rice Council**

Taco Casserole

2 pounds ground beef
1 can (10 ounces) diced tomatoes and green chiles
1 teaspoon salt
1 teaspoon garlic powder
1 teaspoon ground cumin
1 teaspoon paprika
1 teaspoon chili powder
½ teaspoon ground red pepper
½ teaspoon red pepper flakes
1 bag (12 ounces) nacho cheese-flavored tortilla chips, crushed
½ cup chopped green onions
1 cup (4 ounces) shredded Mexican cheese blend
½ cup sour cream (optional)

1. Preheat oven to 375°F.

2. Brown beef in large skillet over medium-high heat 6 to 8 minutes, stirring to break up meat. Drain fat. Stir in tomatoes, salt, garlic powder, cumin, paprika, chili powder, ground red pepper and red pepper flakes; cook 3 minutes.

3. Stir in chips. Transfer to 13×9-inch casserole.

4. Bake 15 to 20 minutes or until heated through. Sprinkle with green onions and cheese. Serve with sour cream, if desired.   Makes 4 to 6 servings

tip

To crush the tortilla chips, simply place the chips in a large resealable food storage bag, then run a rolling pin over the bag several times.

Taco Casserole

Chili Spaghetti Casserole

8 ounces uncooked spaghetti

1 pound ground beef

1 medium onion, chopped

Salt and black pepper

1 can (about 15 ounces) vegetarian chili with beans

1 can (about 14 ounces) Italian-style stewed tomatoes, undrained

1½ cups (6 ounces) shredded sharp Cheddar cheese, divided

½ cup sour cream

1½ teaspoons chili powder

¼ teaspoon garlic powder

1. Preheat oven to 350°F. Spray 13×9-inch baking dish with nonstick cooking spray.

2. Cook spaghetti according to package directions; drain. Place in prepared dish.

3. Meanwhile, place beef and onion in large skillet; season with salt and pepper. Brown beef over medium-high heat 6 to 8 minutes, stirring to break up meat. Drain fat. Stir in chili, tomatoes with juice, 1 cup cheese, sour cream, chili powder and garlic powder.

4. Add chili mixture to spaghetti; stir until spaghetti is well coated. Sprinkle with remaining ½ cup cheese.

5. Bake, covered, 30 minutes or until hot and bubbly. Let stand 5 minutes before serving.

Makes 8 servings

Chili Spaghetti Casserole

Hearty Lasagna Rolls

1½ pounds ground beef
1 cup chopped fresh mushrooms
1 medium onion, finely chopped
1 small carrot, finely chopped
1 clove garlic, finely chopped
¼ cup dry red wine or beef broth
⅛ teaspoon cayenne pepper (optional)
2 cups shredded mozzarella cheese
1 egg, lightly beaten
5 tablespoons grated Parmesan cheese, divided
1 jar (1 pound 8 ounces) RAGÚ® Robusto!® Pasta Sauce
12 ounces lasagna noodles, cooked and drained

1. Preheat oven to 350°F. In 12-inch skillet, brown ground beef over medium-high heat; drain. Stir in mushrooms, onion, carrot and garlic; cook over medium heat, stirring occasionally, until vegetables are tender. Stir in wine and cayenne pepper; cook over high heat 3 minutes. Remove from heat; let stand 10 minutes.

2. In medium bowl, thoroughly combine ground beef mixture, mozzarella cheese, egg and 2 tablespoons Parmesan cheese. In 13×9-inch baking dish, evenly pour 2 cups Pasta Sauce. Evenly spread ⅓ cup ground beef filling over each lasagna noodle. Carefully roll up noodles. Place seam-side-down in baking dish. Evenly spread remaining sauce over lasagna rolls. Bake, covered, 40 minutes. Sprinkle with remaining 3 tablespoons Parmesan cheese and bake, uncovered, 5 minutes or until bubbling.

Makes 6 servings

Hearty Lasagna Rolls

It's a Keeper Casserole

1 tablespoon vegetable oil

½ cup chopped onion

¼ cup chopped green bell pepper

1 clove garlic, minced

2 tablespoons all-purpose flour

1 teaspoon sugar

½ teaspoon salt

½ teaspoon dried basil

½ teaspoon black pepper

1 package (about 16 ounces) frozen meatballs, cooked

1 can (about 14 ounces) whole tomatoes, cut up and drained

1½ cups cooked vegetables (any combination)

1 teaspoon beef bouillon granules

1 teaspoon Worcestershire sauce

1 can (12 ounces) refrigerated buttermilk biscuits

1. Preheat oven to 400°F.

2. Heat oil in large saucepan over medium heat. Add onion, bell pepper and garlic; cook and stir until vegetables are tender. Stir in flour, sugar, salt, basil and black pepper. Add meatballs, tomatoes, vegetables, bouillon and Worcestershire sauce; cook and stir until slightly thickened and bubbly. Pour into 2-quart casserole. Place biscuits on top of casserole.

3. Bake 15 minutes or until biscuits are golden.   Makes 4 servings

Variations: Instead of the frozen meatballs, try beef stew meat or sliced hot dogs.

Layered Pasta Casserole

8 ounces uncooked penne pasta

8 ounces mild Italian sausage, casings removed

8 ounces ground beef

1 jar (about 26 ounces) pasta sauce

1 package (10 ounces) frozen chopped spinach, thawed and squeezed dry

2 cups (8 ounces) shredded mozzarella cheese, divided

1 cup ricotta cheese

½ cup grated Parmesan cheese

1 egg

2 tablespoons chopped fresh basil *or* 2 teaspoons dried basil

1 teaspoon salt

1. Preheat oven to 350°F. Spray 13×9-inch baking dish with nonstick cooking spray.

2. Cook pasta according to package directions; drain. Transfer to prepared dish.

3. Brown sausage and beef in large skillet over medium-high heat 6 to 8 minutes, stirring to break up meat. Drain fat. Add pasta sauce; mix well. Add half of meat sauce to pasta; toss to coat.

4. Combine spinach, 1 cup mozzarella cheese, ricotta cheese, Parmesan cheese, egg, basil and salt in medium bowl. Spoon small mounds of spinach mixture over pasta mixture; spread evenly with back of spoon. Top with remaining meat sauce; sprinkle with remaining 1 cup mozzarella cheese.

5. Bake 30 minutes or until heated through.   Makes 6 to 8 servings

Layered Pasta Casserole

Speedy Sirloin Steak Casserole

1 (1½-pound) beef top sirloin steak, cut 1 inch thick

2 tablespoons extra virgin olive oil, divided

1 sheet refrigerated pie dough

1 teaspoon dried dill weed

½ teaspoon salt

1 medium onion, coarsely chopped

½ pound mushrooms, cut into quarters

1 tablespoon all-purpose flour

½ cup milk

1 teaspoon ground nutmeg

1 teaspoon beef bouillon granules

8 ounces (2 cups) shredded JARLSBERG® cheese

2 cups frozen peas

Cut beef into ¼-inch-thick slices. Cut each slice into 1-inch pieces. Combine with 1 tablespoon oil. Allow pie dough to stand at room temperature as package directs.

Heat large nonstick skillet until hot. Stir-fry beef mixture (half at a time) 1 to 2 minutes. Remove from skillet. Combine beef mixture, dill and salt; set aside.

Heat remaining 1 tablespoon oil in same skillet; add onion and cook until softened, about 3 to 4 minutes. Add mushrooms; cook 5 minutes, stirring frequently. Sprinkle with flour; cook 1 minute. Add milk, nutmeg and bouillon. Bring mixture to a boil and cook, stirring constantly, until mixture thickens. Add cheese; mix lightly until cheese melts. Stir in reserved beef mixture with accumulated juices and peas.

Spoon mixture into round 2-quart casserole. Fold pie crust edges under to fit inside edge of casserole; place on top of meat mixture. Crimp edges decoratively and cut slits in several places near center (to prevent cracking). Bake casserole in preheated 450°F oven 10 to 12 minutes or until crust is browned.   Makes 6 servings

Prep Time: 30 minutes
Bake Time: 10 to 12 minutes

Easy Vegetable Beef Stew

1 pound beef stew meat

1 can (about 14 ounces) diced tomatoes

1 onion, cut into 8 wedges

4 carrots, cut into 1-inch pieces

1 green or red bell pepper, diced

1 stalk celery, sliced

1 teaspoon Italian seasoning

   Salt and black pepper

1 tablespoon vegetable oil

1 package (8 ounces) sliced mushrooms

1. Preheat oven to 325°F. Combine beef, tomatoes and onion in Dutch oven.

2. Bake, covered, 1 hour.

3. Add carrots, bell pepper, celery, Italian seasoning, salt and black pepper to beef mixture; stir.

4. Bake, covered, 45 minutes or until beef and carrots are tender.

5. Heat oil in large skillet over medium heat. Add mushrooms; cook and stir 10 minutes or until lightly browned and tender. Stir mushrooms into stew.

Makes 4 servings

Variation: Two unpeeled medium red potatoes, cut into 2-inch pieces, can be added with the carrots.

Pizza Roll-Ups

½ pound lean ground beef or turkey
1 small onion, chopped
¾ teaspoon garlic salt
¼ teaspoon crushed red pepper flakes
1 jar (28 ounces) pasta sauce with mushrooms, divided
2 cups (8 ounces) SARGENTO® Fancy Shredded 6 Cheese Italian Cheese, divided
8 long (6 ounces) lasagna noodles, cooked and drained

1. Brown ground beef and onion in large skillet. Pour off drippings. Sprinkle meat mixture with garlic salt and pepper flakes. Remove from heat; stir in ½ cup pasta sauce and 1½ cups cheese.

2. Spoon 1 cup pasta sauce into 2-quart rectangular baking dish. Spoon ¼ cup meat mixture down center of each lasagna noodle; roll up and place, seam-side down, in baking dish. Spoon remaining sauce over roll-ups.

3. Cover with foil; bake in preheated 375°F oven 35 minutes or until heated through. Remove from oven; uncover and sprinkle with remaining cheese. Let stand 5 minutes before serving.

Makes 8 servings

Prep Time: 20 minutes
Bake Time: 35 minutes

Barney's Colorful Casserole

6 potatoes, thinly sliced
6 to 8 carrots, thinly sliced
2 onions, thinly sliced
    Salt and black pepper
1 can (46 ounces) tomato juice
1 can (10 ounces) diced tomatoes and green chiles
16 cooked meatballs

1. Preheat oven to 375°F. Spray 13×9-inch baking pan with nonstick cooking spray.

2. Arrange potatoes, carrots and onions in single overlapping layer in prepared pan. Season with salt and pepper. Heat tomato juice and tomatoes in small saucepan over medium heat; pour over vegetables.

3. Bake 1½ hours or until vegetables are tender. Top with meatballs; bake 15 minutes or until browned.

Makes 8 servings

Zucchini Parmigiana Casserole

½ cup all-purpose flour

3 eggs, beaten

2 cups Italian-seasoned dry bread crumbs

6 cups sliced zucchini

½ cup olive oil

Salt and black pepper

1 pound ground beef

½ pound bulk pork sausage

1 cup chopped onion

1 tablespoon minced garlic

¼ cup chopped fresh basil

¼ cup chopped fresh oregano

4 cups tomato sauce

2 cups (8 ounces) shredded mozzarella cheese

¼ cup grated Parmesan cheese

¼ cup chopped fresh parsley

1. Preheat oven to 350°F.

2. Place flour, eggs and bread crumbs in separate small shallow bowls. Dip zucchini in flour, eggs, then bread crumbs to coat. Heat oil in medium skillet over medium-high heat. Brown zucchini on both sides in batches; season with salt and pepper. Drain on paper towels. Discard oil.

3. Add ground beef, sausage, onion and garlic to same skillet; cook 6 to 8 minutes or until meat is cooked through, stirring to break up meat. Drain fat. Stir in basil and oregano.

4. Layer half of tomato sauce, half of zucchini, half of meat mixture, half of mozzarella cheese and half of Parmesan cheese in 4-quart casserole. Repeat layers.

5. Bake 30 minutes or until heated through and cheese is melted. Top with parsley.

Makes 6 servings

Rigatoni à la Vodka

    1 pound ground beef
    1 jar (26 ounces) pasta sauce
1½ cups 3-cheese pasta sauce
    4 cups (16 ounces) shredded mozzarella and Cheddar cheese blend, divided
    ¼ cup plus 2 tablespoons vodka
12 ounces rigatoni pasta, cooked and drained

1. Preheat oven to 350°F. Spray 3-quart casserole with nonstick cooking spray. Brown beef in large skillet over medium heat 6 to 8 minutes, stirring to break up meat. Drain fat. Add pasta sauces, 2 cups cheese and vodka; cook and stir until heated through.

2. Place pasta in prepared casserole. Pour vodka sauce evenly over pasta; sprinkle with remaining 2 cups cheese.

3. Bake 15 minutes or until cheese is melted.   Makes 4 servings

Zesty Italian Stuffed Peppers

    3 bell peppers (green, red or yellow)
    1 pound ground beef
    1 jar (14 ounces) spaghetti sauce
1⅓ cups FRENCH'S® French Fried Onions, divided
    2 tablespoons FRANK'S® REDHOT® Original Cayenne Pepper Sauce
    ½ cup uncooked instant rice
    ¼ cup sliced ripe olives
    1 cup (4 ounces) shredded mozzarella cheese

1. Preheat oven to 400°F. Cut bell peppers in half lengthwise through stems; discard seeds. Place pepper halves, cut sides up, in shallow 2-quart baking dish; set aside.

2. Place beef in large microwavable bowl. Microwave on HIGH 5 minutes or until meat is browned, stirring once. Drain. Stir in spaghetti sauce, ⅔ *cup* French Fried Onions, Frank's RedHot Sauce, rice and olives. Spoon evenly into bell pepper halves.

3. Cover; bake 35 minutes or until bell peppers are tender. Uncover; sprinkle with cheese and remaining ⅔ *cup* onions. Bake 1 minute or until onions are golden brown.   Makes 6 servings

Prep Time: 10 minutes
Bake Time: 36 minutes

Beef Pot Pie with Beer Biscuits

4 **bacon slices, coarsely chopped**
2½ **pounds beef chuck, cut into 1-inch cubes**
2¼ **teaspoons salt, divided**
½ **teaspoon black pepper**
1 **large onion, chopped**
3 **carrots, cut into ½-inch rounds**
3 **celery stalks, cut into ½-inch rounds**
2 **cloves garlic, minced**
2⅓ **cups plus 1 tablespoon all-purpose flour, divided**
1 **can (about 14 ounces) beef broth**
2 **tablespoons Worcestershire sauce**
1 **teaspoon dried thyme**
2½ **teaspoons baking powder**
6 **tablespoons unsalted butter, cut into ½-inch cubes**
¾ **cup lager**

1. Preheat oven to 350°F.

2. Cook bacon in Dutch oven over medium heat until crisp and browned. Transfer to paper towels using slotted spoon. Reserve 2 tablespoons fat in Dutch oven.

3. Season beef with 1½ teaspoons salt and pepper; add to Dutch oven in batches. Cook and stir over medium-high heat 5 minutes or until browned. Transfer to plate using slotted spoon; reserve fat in Dutch oven.

4. Add onion, carrots, celery and garlic; cook and stir over medium heat 5 minutes or until vegetables are tender. Sprinkle with ⅓ cup plus 1 tablespoon flour; stir well. Stir in bacon, beef, broth, Worcestershire sauce and thyme; bring to a boil.

5. Bake, covered, 1½ hours or until beef is almost tender.

6. For biscuits, whisk remaining 2 cups flour, baking powder and remaining ¾ teaspoon salt in medium bowl. Cut in butter with pastry blender or two knives until mixture resembles coarse crumbs. Stir in enough lager to make soft dough. Turn dough out onto lightly floured work surface. Roll dough into 9×6-inch rectangle about ½ inch thick. Cut into six 3-inch square biscuits.

7. Remove Dutch oven from oven. *Increase oven temperature to 400°F.* Place biscuits over stew, overlapping if needed. Bake 20 minutes or until biscuits are golden brown.

Makes 6 servings

Rainbow Casserole

5 potatoes, peeled and cut into thin slices
1 pound ground beef
1 onion, halved and thinly sliced
   Salt and black pepper
1 can (about 28 ounces) stewed tomatoes, drained, juice reserved
1 cup frozen peas *or* 1 can (about 6 ounces) peas, drained

1. Preheat oven to 350°F. Lightly coat 3-quart casserole with nonstick cooking spray.

2. Combine potatoes and enough water to cover in large saucepan; bring to a boil over high heat. Reduce heat to low; simmer 15 minutes or until almost tender. Drain. Meanwhile, brown beef in large skillet over medium-high heat 6 to 8 minutes, stirring to break up meat. Drain fat.

3. Layer half of beef, half of potatoes, half of onion, salt, pepper, half of tomatoes and half of peas in prepared casserole. Repeat layers. Add reserved tomato juice.

4. Bake, covered, 40 minutes or until most liquid is absorbed.

Makes 4 to 6 servings

Au Gratin Beef Bake

1 pound ground beef
1 package (26 ounces) shredded hash browns
¾ cup sour cream
1 teaspoon salt
1 teaspoon black pepper
½ cup chopped onion
¾ cup grated mozzarella cheese
¾ cup grated Cheddar cheese, divided
1 pint whipping cream
1 can black olives

Preheat oven to 350°F. Mix hash browns with sour cream, salt and pepper; place in 13×9-inch pan. Brown ground beef with chopped onion. Drain. Combine mozzarella cheese with ½ cup Cheddar cheese; add to beef. Place beef mixture over hash browns. Pour cream over beef mixture. Bake 25 minutes. Remove from oven and top with remaining Cheddar cheese and olives. Bake an additional 10 minutes.

Makes 4 to 6 servings

Favorite recipe from **North Dakota Beef Commission**

Rainbow Casserole

Pizza Casserole

2 cups uncooked rotini or other spiral pasta
1½ pounds ground beef
1 medium onion, chopped
   Salt and black pepper
1 can (about 15 ounces) pizza sauce
1 can (8 ounces) tomato sauce
1 can (6 ounces) tomato paste
½ teaspoon sugar
½ teaspoon garlic salt
½ teaspoon dried oregano
2 cups (8 ounces) shredded mozzarella cheese
12 to 15 slices pepperoni

1. Preheat oven to 350°F.

2. Cook pasta according to package directions; drain.

3. Meanwhile, brown beef with onion in large skillet over medium-high heat 6 to 8 minutes, stirring to break up meat. Drain fat. Season with salt and pepper.

4. Combine pasta, pizza sauce, tomato sauce, tomato paste, sugar, garlic salt and oregano in large bowl. Add beef mixture; stir until blended.

5. Place half of mixture in ovenproof skillet or 3-quart casserole; top with 1 cup cheese. Repeat layers. Arrange pepperoni slices on top.

6. Bake 25 to 30 minutes or until heated through and cheese is melted.

Makes 6 servings

tip

The next time you're making a casserole, assemble and bake two. Allow one to cool completely, then wrap it in heavy-duty foil and freeze for another day. To reheat a frozen 3-quart casserole, unwrap it and microwave, covered, on HIGH 30 to 40 minutes. Allow to stand about 5 minutes before serving.

Spinach-Potato Bake

1 pound ground beef
1 small onion, chopped
½ cup sliced mushrooms
2 cloves garlic, minced
1 package (10 ounces) frozen chopped spinach, thawed and squeezed dry
½ teaspoon ground nutmeg
1 pound russet potatoes, peeled, cooked and mashed
¼ cup sour cream
¼ cup milk
Salt and black pepper
½ cup (2 ounces) shredded Cheddar cheese

1. Preheat oven to 400°F. Lightly coat 9-inch baking dish with nonstick cooking spray.

2. Brown beef in large nonstick skillet over medium-high heat 6 to 8 minutes, stirring to break up meat. Drain all but 1 tablespoon fat. Add onion, mushrooms and garlic; cook and stir until tender. Stir in spinach and nutmeg; cook until heated through, stirring occasionally.

3. Combine potatoes, sour cream and milk in medium bowl. Add to beef mixture; season with salt and pepper. Spoon into prepared baking dish; sprinkle with cheese.

4. Bake 15 to 20 minutes or until slightly puffed and cheese is melted.

Makes 6 servings

Spinach-Potato Bake

Beef in Wine Sauce

4 pounds boneless beef chuck roast, cut into 1½- to 2-inch cubes
2 tablespoons garlic powder
2 cans (10¾ ounces each) condensed golden mushroom soup, undiluted
1 can (8 ounces) sliced mushrooms, drained
¾ cup dry sherry
1 package (about 1 ounce) dry onion soup mix
1 bag (20 ounces) frozen sliced carrots, thawed

1. Preheat oven to 325°F. Spray heavy 4-quart casserole or Dutch oven with nonstick cooking spray.

2. Sprinkle beef with garlic powder. Place in prepared casserole.

3. Combine canned soup, mushrooms, sherry and dry soup mix in medium bowl. Pour over meat; mix well.

4. Bake, covered, 3 hours or until meat is tender. Add carrots during last 15 minutes of cooking.   Makes 6 to 8 servings

Cheeseburger to the Max

1½ pounds lean ground beef
½ cup ketchup
2 tablespoons FRENCH'S® Worcestershire Sauce
1 egg, beaten
1⅓ cups FRENCH'S® French Fried Onions, divided
6 slices American cheese
½ cup crumbled cooked bacon

1. Preheat oven to 350°F. Combine ground beef, ketchup, Worcestershire, egg and ⅔ *cup* French Fried Onions until well mixed.

2. Shape beef mixture into 8-inch round burger on pizza pan or jelly-roll pan. Bake 40 minutes or until no longer pink in center and juices run clear.

3. Top with cheese, bacon and remaining ⅔ *cup* onions. Bake 5 minutes or until cheese is melted and onions are golden.   Makes 6 servings

Prep Time: 10 minutes
Bake Time: 45 minutes

Beef in Wine Sauce

Beef Stroganoff Casserole

1 pound ground beef
Salt and black pepper
1 teaspoon vegetable oil
8 ounces sliced mushrooms
1 large onion, chopped
3 cloves garlic, minced
¼ cup dry white wine
1 can (10¾ ounces) condensed cream of mushroom soup, undiluted
½ cup sour cream
1 tablespoon Dijon mustard
4 cups cooked egg noodles
Chopped fresh parsley (optional)

1. Preheat oven to 350°F. Spray 13×9-inch baking dish with nonstick cooking spray.

2. Place beef in large skillet; season with salt and pepper. Brown beef over medium-high heat 6 to 8 minutes, stirring to break up meat. Drain fat. Remove beef from skillet and set aside.

3. Heat oil in same skillet over medium-high heat. Add mushrooms, onion and garlic; cook and stir 2 minutes or until onion is tender. Add wine. Reduce heat to medium-low and simmer 3 minutes. Remove from heat; stir in soup, sour cream and mustard until well blended. Return beef to skillet; stir to blend.

4. Place noodles in prepared dish. Pour beef mixture over noodles; stir until noodles are well coated.

5. Bake 30 minutes or until heated through. Sprinkle with parsley, if desired.

Makes 6 servings

Beef Stroganoff Casserole

Rice Lasagna

Nonstick cooking spray

1 cup MINUTE® White Rice, uncooked

2 eggs, lightly beaten

¾ cup grated Parmesan cheese, divided

2 cups shredded mozzarella cheese

½ cup cottage cheese

1 pound lean ground beef

1 jar (15½ ounces) spaghetti sauce

½ teaspoon garlic powder

PREHEAT oven to 375°F. Coat 13×9-inch baking dish with nonstick cooking spray.

PREPARE rice according to package directions. Cool slightly.

COMBINE rice, eggs and ¼ cup Parmesan cheese in medium bowl. Mix well; set aside. Combine ¼ cup Parmesan cheese, mozzarella cheese and cottage cheese in separate bowl. Mix well; set aside. Spray large nonstick skillet with nonstick cooking spray.

ADD beef and brown over medium heat; drain off excess fat. Add spaghetti sauce and garlic powder; continue cooking until thoroughly heated.

SPOON one-half of rice mixture into baking dish. Cover with one-half of cheese mixture. Top with one-half of meat sauce. Repeat layers. Top with remaining ¼ cup Parmesan cheese.

BAKE 15 to 20 minutes or until thoroughly heated.   Makes 6 to 8 servings

Italian-Style Shepherd's Pie

1 pound potatoes, peeled and quartered

2 to 3 tablespoons chicken broth

3 tablespoons grated Parmesan cheese

1 pound ground beef

½ cup chopped onion

2 teaspoons Italian seasoning

⅛ teaspoon ground red pepper

2 cups sliced yellow summer squash

1 can (about 14 ounces) Italian-style tomatoes, drained

1 cup frozen corn

⅓ cup tomato paste

1. Preheat oven to 375°F.

2. Combine potatoes and enough water to cover in medium saucepan; bring to a boil. Boil, uncovered, 20 to 25 minutes or until tender; drain. Mash potatoes, adding enough broth to reach desired consistency. Stir in cheese.

3. Brown beef and onion in large skillet over medium-high heat 6 to 8 minutes, stirring to break up meat. Drain fat. Stir in Italian seasoning and red pepper. Add squash, tomatoes, corn and tomato paste; mix well. Spoon mixture into 2-quart casserole. Pipe or spoon potatoes over top.

4. Bake 20 to 25 minutes or until meat mixture is bubbly. Let stand 10 minutes before serving.

Makes 6 servings

Manicotti

1 container (15 ounces) ricotta cheese
2 cups (8 ounces) shredded mozzarella cheese
½ cup cottage cheese
2 eggs, beaten
2 tablespoons grated Parmesan cheese
½ teaspoon minced garlic
   Salt and black pepper
1 package (about 8 ounces) uncooked manicotti shells
1 pound ground beef
1 jar (about 26 ounces) pasta sauce
2 cups water

1. Preheat oven to 375°F.

2. Combine ricotta cheese, mozzarella cheese, cottage cheese, eggs, Parmesan cheese, garlic, salt and pepper in large bowl; mix well. Fill manicotti shells with cheese mixture; place in 13×9-inch baking dish.

3. Brown beef in large skillet over medium-high heat 6 to 8 minutes, stirring to break up meat. Drain fat. Stir in pasta sauce and water. Pour sauce over filled manicotti shells.

4. Bake, covered, 1 hour or until sauce is thickened and shells are tender.

Makes 6 servings

Reuben Noodle Bake

8 ounces uncooked egg noodles
5 ounces thinly sliced deli-style corned beef
2 cups (8 ounces) shredded Swiss cheese
1 can (14 ounces) sauerkraut with caraway seeds, drained
½ cup Thousand Island dressing
½ cup milk
1 tablespoon prepared mustard
2 slices pumpernickel bread
1 tablespoon butter, melted

1. Preheat oven to 350°F. Spray 13×9-inch baking dish with nonstick cooking spray.

2. Cook noodles according to package directions; drain.

3. Meanwhile, cut corned beef into bite-size pieces. Combine noodles, corned beef, cheese and sauerkraut in large bowl. Transfer to prepared baking dish.

4. Combine dressing, milk and mustard in small bowl. Spoon evenly over noodle mixture.

5. Tear bread into large pieces; process in food processor or blender until crumbs form. Combine bread crumbs and butter in small bowl; sprinkle evenly over casserole.

6. Bake 25 to 30 minutes or until heated through.   Makes 6 servings

tip

Sauerkraut is chopped or shredded cabbage that has been salted and fermented. Always drain sauerkraut before using in casseroles or on sandwiches.

Reuben Noodle Bake

Summer Fiesta Casserole

2 pounds ground beef
1 medium onion, chopped
1 package (about 1 ounce) taco seasoning mix
4 to 6 potatoes, peeled and cut into ½-inch cubes (about 4 cups)
1 to 2 tablespoons vegetable oil
4 cups sliced zucchini
1 can (about 14 ounces) diced tomatoes with onion and garlic
1½ cups (6 ounces) shredded Mexican cheese blend

1. Preheat oven to 350°F. Spray 4-quart casserole with nonstick cooking spray.

2. Brown beef and onion in large skillet over medium heat 6 to 8 minutes, stirring to break up meat. Drain fat. Add taco seasoning and cook 5 minutes, stirring occasionally. Transfer meat mixture to prepared casserole.

3. Add potatoes to same skillet; cook and stir over medium heat until potatoes are browned, adding oil as needed to prevent sticking. Add zucchini; cook and stir until beginning to soften. Transfer to casserole; top with tomatoes and cheese.

4. Bake 10 to 15 minutes or until cheese is melted and casserole is heated through.

Makes 4 to 6 servings

Serving Suggestions: Serve with tortilla chips, sour cream and/or salsa.

Meat Crust Pie

    1 pound ground beef
    2 cans (8 ounces each) tomato sauce, divided
    ½ cup seasoned dry bread crumbs
    ½ cup chopped green bell pepper, divided
    ¼ cup minced onion
    1 teaspoon salt, divided
    ⅛ teaspoon dried oregano
    ⅛ teaspoon black pepper
    1 cup water
 1⅓ cups uncooked instant rice
    1 cup (4 ounces) shredded Cheddar cheese, divided

1. Preheat oven to 350°F.

2. Combine beef, ½ cup tomato sauce, bread crumbs, ¼ cup bell pepper, onion, ½ teaspoon salt, oregano and black pepper in large bowl; mix well. Pat onto bottom and up side of ungreased 9-inch deep-dish pie plate.

3. Bring water and remaining ½ teaspoon salt to a boil in medium saucepan. Stir in rice; cover and remove from heat. Let stand 5 minutes or until water is absorbed. Add remaining 1½ cups tomato sauce, ½ cup cheese and remaining ¼ cup bell pepper to rice; mix well. Spoon rice mixture into meat crust.

4. Bake, covered, 25 minutes. Remove from oven and drain fat carefully, holding pan lid over top to keep pie from sliding. Top with remaining ½ cup cheese. Bake, uncovered, 10 to 15 minutes or until cheese is melted. Carefully drain fat again.

Makes 8 servings

Meat Crust Pie

Oven-Baked Stew

2 pounds boneless beef chuck or round steak, cut into 1-inch cubes
¼ cup all-purpose flour
1⅓ cups sliced carrots
1 can (14 to 16 ounces) whole peeled tomatoes, undrained and chopped
1 envelope LIPTON® RECIPE SECRETS® Onion Soup Mix*
½ cup dry red wine or water
1 cup fresh or canned sliced mushrooms
1 package (8 ounces) medium or broad egg noodles, cooked and drained

Also terrific with LIPTON® RECIPE SECRETS® Beefy Onion or Onion Mushroom Soup Mix.

1. Preheat oven to 425°F. In 2½-quart shallow casserole, toss beef with flour, then bake, uncovered, 20 minutes, stirring once.

2. *Reduce heat to 350°F.* Stir in carrots, tomatoes, soup mix and wine.

3. Bake, covered, 1½ hours or until beef is tender. Stir in mushrooms and bake, covered, an additional 10 minutes. Serve over hot noodles.   Makes 8 servings

Prep Time: 20 minutes
Bake Time: 2 hours

Hearty Beef and Potato Casserole

1 package (about 17 ounces) refrigerated fully cooked beef pot roast in gravy*
3 cups frozen hash brown potatoes
   Salt and black pepper
1 can (about 14 ounces) diced tomatoes
½ cup canned chipotle chile sauce
1 cup (4 ounces) shredded sharp Cheddar cheese

Fully cooked beef pot roast in gravy can be found in the refrigerated prepared meats section of the supermarket.

1. Preheat oven to 375°F. Spray 11×7-inch baking dish with nonstick cooking spray.

2. Drain and discard gravy from pot roast. Cut beef into ¼-inch-thick slices. Place 2 cups potatoes in prepared baking dish. Sprinkle with salt and pepper. Top with beef. Combine tomatoes and chile sauce in small bowl; spread evenly over beef. Top with remaining 1 cup potatoes. Sprinkle with cheese.

3. Bake, covered, 20 minutes. Bake, uncovered, 20 minutes or until hot and bubbly. Let stand 5 minutes before serving.   Makes 6 servings

Cousin Arlene's Spaghetti Lasagna

8 ounces uncooked spaghetti

1 tablespoon butter

1 clove garlic, minced

2 pounds ground beef

1 teaspoon sugar

Salt and black pepper

2 cans (8 ounces each) tomato sauce

1 can (6 ounces) tomato paste

1 cup (8 ounces) sour cream

3 ounces cream cheese, softened

6 green onions, chopped

¼ cup grated Parmesan cheese

1. Preheat oven to 350°F.

2. Cook spaghetti according to package directions; drain.

3. Meanwhile, melt butter in large skillet over medium heat. Add garlic; cook and stir 1 minute. Add ground beef, sugar, salt and pepper. Brown beef 6 to 8 minutes, stirring to break up meat. Drain fat. Add tomato sauce and tomato paste; simmer 20 minutes, stirring occasionally.

4. Meanwhile, beat sour cream and cream cheese in medium bowl until smooth. Stir in green onions.

5. Spread ½ cup meat sauce in 2-quart casserole. Layer with half of spaghetti, half of sour cream mixture and half of remaining meat sauce. Repeat layers. Sprinkle with Parmesan cheese.

6. Bake 35 minutes or until heated through.   Makes 6 servings

Chicken-Asparagus Casserole

2 teaspoons vegetable oil

1 cup chopped green and/or red bell peppers

1 medium onion, chopped

2 cloves garlic, minced

1 can (10¾ ounces) condensed cream of asparagus soup, undiluted

1 container (8 ounces) ricotta cheese

2 cups (8 ounces) shredded Cheddar cheese, divided

2 eggs

1½ cups chopped cooked chicken

1 package (10 ounces) frozen chopped asparagus,* thawed and drained

8 ounces egg noodles, cooked and drained

Black pepper (optional)

Or substitute ½ pound fresh asparagus cut into ½-inch pieces. Bring 6 cups water to a boil in large saucepan over high heat. Add asparagus. Reduce heat to medium. Cook, covered, 5 to 8 minutes or until crisp-tender. Drain.

1. Preheat oven to 350°F. Grease 13×9-inch casserole.

2. Heat oil in small skillet over medium heat. Add bell peppers, onion and garlic; cook and stir until vegetables are crisp-tender.

3. Mix soup, ricotta cheese, 1 cup Cheddar cheese and eggs in large bowl until well blended. Add onion mixture, chicken, asparagus and noodles; mix well. Season with black pepper, if desired.

4. Spread mixture evenly in prepared casserole. Top with remaining 1 cup Cheddar cheese.

5. Bake 30 minutes or until center is set and cheese is bubbly. Let stand 5 minutes before serving. Makes 12 servings

Chicken Cassoulet

4 slices bacon
¼ cup all-purpose flour
Salt and black pepper
1¾ pounds bone-in chicken pieces
2 chicken sausages (2¼ ounces each), cooked and cut into ¼-inch pieces
1 medium onion, chopped
1½ cups diced red and green bell peppers
2 cloves garlic, minced
1 teaspoon dried thyme
Olive oil
2 cans (about 15 ounces each) cannellini or Great Northern beans, rinsed and drained
½ cup dry white wine (optional)

1. Preheat oven to 350°F.

2. Cook bacon in large skillet over medium-high heat until crisp; drain on paper towels. Cut into 1-inch pieces. Pour off all but 2 tablespoons fat from skillet.

3. Place flour in shallow bowl; season with salt and black pepper. Dip chicken pieces in flour mixture; shake off excess. Brown chicken in batches in skillet over medium-high heat; remove to plate. Lightly brown sausages in same skillet; remove to plate.

4. Add onion, bell peppers, garlic and thyme to skillet; cook and stir over medium heat 5 minutes or until softened, adding oil as needed to prevent sticking. Transfer onion mixture to 13×9-inch baking dish. Add beans; mix well. Add bacon, chicken and sausages. Add wine to skillet, if desired; cook and stir over medium heat, scraping up browned bits from bottom of skillet. Pour over casserole.

5. Bake, covered, 40 minutes. Bake, uncovered, 15 minutes or until chicken is cooked through (165°F).

Makes 6 servings

Chicken Cassoulet

Dairyland Confetti Chicken

1 cup diced carrots
¾ cup chopped onion
½ cup diced celery
¼ cup chicken broth
3 cups cubed cooked chicken
1 can (10½ ounces) cream of chicken soup, undiluted
1 cup dairy sour cream
½ cup (4 ounces) sliced mushrooms
1 teaspoon Worcestershire sauce
1 teaspoon salt
⅛ teaspoon black pepper
Confetti Topping (recipe follows)
¼ cup (1 ounce) shredded Wisconsin Cheddar cheese

For casserole, in saucepan, combine carrots, onion, celery and chicken broth. Simmer 20 minutes. In 3-quart casserole, mix cubed chicken, soup, sour cream, mushrooms, Worcestershire sauce, salt and pepper. Add simmered vegetables and liquid; mix well. Prepare Confetti Topping. Drop tablespoons of Confetti Topping onto casserole. Bake in 350°F oven for 40 to 45 minutes or until golden brown. Sprinkle with cheese and return to oven until melted. Garnish as desired.

Makes 6 to 8 servings

Confetti Topping

1 cup sifted all-purpose flour
2 teaspoons baking powder
½ teaspoon salt
2 eggs, lightly beaten
½ cup milk
1 tablespoon chopped green bell pepper
1 tablespoon chopped pimiento
1 cup (4 ounces) shredded Wisconsin Cheddar cheese

In mixing bowl, combine flour, baking powder and salt. Add eggs, milk, green pepper, pimiento and cheese. Mix just until well blended.   Makes about 2 cups

Favorite recipe from **Wisconsin Milk Marketing Board**

Dairyland Confetti Chicken

Wild Rice & Chicken Casserole

1 package (6 ounces) long grain & wild rice mix
2 tablespoons butter
½ cup chopped onion
½ cup chopped celery
2 cups cubed cooked chicken
1 can (10¾ ounces) condensed cream of mushroom soup, undiluted
½ cup sour cream
⅓ cup dry white wine
½ teaspoon curry powder

1. Preheat oven to 350°F.

2. Prepare rice mix according to package directions.

3. Meanwhile, melt butter in large skillet over medium heat. Add onion and celery; cook and stir until tender. Stir in rice, chicken, soup, sour cream, wine and curry powder. Transfer mixture to 2-quart casserole.

4. Bake 40 minutes or until heated through.   Makes 4 to 6 servings

tip

Purchase a rotisserie chicken from your local supermarket for dinner one night and use 2 cups leftover chicken to make this delicious Wild Rice & Chicken Casserole the next.

Wild Rice & Chicken Casserole

Chicken Marsala

6 ounces uncooked wide egg noodles

½ cup Italian-seasoned dry bread crumbs

1 teaspoon dried basil

1 egg

1 teaspoon water

4 boneless skinless chicken breasts

3 tablespoons olive oil, divided

¾ cup chopped onion

8 ounces cremini or button mushrooms, sliced

3 cloves garlic, minced

3 tablespoons all-purpose flour

1 can (about 14 ounces) chicken broth

½ cup dry marsala wine

    Salt and black pepper

    Chopped fresh parsley (optional)

1. Preheat oven to 375°F. Spray 11×7-inch baking dish with nonstick cooking spray.

2. Cook noodles according to package directions; drain. Place in prepared dish.

3. Meanwhile, combine bread crumbs and basil in shallow dish. Beat egg and water in another shallow dish. Dip chicken in egg mixture; shake off excess. Dip chicken in crumb mixture; turn and pat to coat.

4. Heat 2 tablespoons oil in large skillet over medium-high heat. Cook chicken 3 minutes per side or until browned. Transfer to plate.

5. Heat remaining 1 tablespoon oil in same skillet over medium heat. Add onion; cook and stir 5 minutes. Add mushrooms and garlic; cook and stir 3 minutes. Sprinkle mushroom mixture with flour; cook and stir 1 minute. Add broth, wine, salt and pepper; bring to a boil over high heat. Cook and stir 5 minutes or until sauce thickens.

6. Reserve ½ cup sauce. Pour remaining sauce over noodles; stir until noodles are well coated. Place chicken on top of noodles. Spoon reserved sauce over chicken.

7. Bake 20 minutes or until chicken is no longer pink in center and sauce is bubbly. Sprinkle with parsley, if desired.   Makes 4 servings

Serving Suggestions: Serve with crusty Italian or French bread and a tossed salad.

Chicken Noodle Casserole

1 package (12 ounces) uncooked wide egg noodles
2 cups chopped cooked chicken
1 can (10¾ ounces) condensed cream of mushroom soup, undiluted
1 cup (4 ounces) shredded Cheddar-Jack cheese
½ cup sour cream
½ cup milk
⅓ to ½ cup plain dry bread crumbs
1 to 2 tablespoons chopped fresh parsley (optional)

1. Preheat oven to 350°F. Spray 13×9-inch baking pan with nonstick cooking spray.

2. Cook noodles according to package directions; drain. Return to saucepan. Add chicken, soup, cheese, sour cream and milk; mix well. Transfer to prepared pan; top with bread crumbs.

3. Bake 25 minutes or until hot and bubbly. Garnish with parsley.

Makes 4 to 6 servings

Homestyle Chicken & Rice Casserole

1 cup long grain white rice
1 can (14 ounces) chicken broth
¾ cup chopped onion
2 cups small broccoli florets
4 (2½ pounds) bone-in chicken breast halves
1 teaspoon paprika
1 teaspoon thyme leaves
1 teaspoon garlic salt
2 cups (8 ounces) SARGENTO® Fancy Shredded Mild Cheddar Cheese

1. Combine rice, broth, onion and broccoli in 11×7-inch baking pan. Place chicken over rice mixture. Combine paprika, thyme and garlic salt in small bowl; sprinkle over chicken.

2. Cover with foil; bake in preheated 375°F oven 40 minutes. Uncover; bake 15 minutes more or until liquid is absorbed, rice is tender and chicken is cooked through.

3. Sprinkle chicken and rice with cheese. Bake 5 minutes more or until cheese is melted.

Makes 4 servings

Prep Time: 15 minutes
Bake Time: 60 minutes

Chicken Noodle Casserole

Chicken Divan Casserole

1 cup uncooked rice
1 cup coarsely shredded carrots
1 tablespoon olive oil
4 boneless skinless chicken breasts
2 tablespoons butter
3 tablespoons all-purpose flour
   Salt and black pepper
1 cup chicken broth
½ cup milk or half-and-half
¼ cup dry white wine
⅓ cup plus 2 tablespoons grated Parmesan cheese, divided
1 pound frozen broccoli florets

1. Preheat oven to 350°F. Spray 13×9-inch baking dish with nonstick cooking spray.

2. Prepare rice according to package directions. Stir in carrots. Spread mixture in prepared baking dish.

3. Heat oil in large skillet over medium-high heat. Brown chicken about 2 minutes on each side. Arrange over rice.

4. To prepare sauce, melt butter in medium saucepan over medium heat. Whisk in flour, salt and pepper; cook and stir 1 minute. Gradually whisk in broth and milk; cook and stir until mixture comes to a boil. Reduce heat; simmer 2 minutes. Stir in wine. Remove from heat. Stir in ⅓ cup cheese.

5. Arrange broccoli around chicken. Pour sauce over top. Sprinkle remaining 2 tablespoons cheese over chicken.

6. Bake, covered, 30 minutes. Bake, uncovered, 10 to 15 minutes or until chicken is no longer pink in center.

Makes 6 servings

Chicken, Asparagus & Mushroom Bake

1 tablespoon butter

1 tablespoon olive oil

2 boneless skinless chicken breasts (about ½ pound),
   cut into bite-size pieces

2 cloves garlic, minced

1 cup sliced mushrooms

2 cups sliced asparagus

   Black pepper

1 package (about 6 ounces) corn bread stuffing mix

¼ cup dry white wine (optional)

1 can (about 14 ounces) chicken broth

1 can (10¾ ounces) condensed cream of asparagus or
   cream of chicken soup, undiluted

1. Preheat oven to 350°F.

2. Heat butter and oil in large skillet over medium-high heat. Add chicken and garlic; cook and stir 3 minutes or until chicken is browned. Add mushrooms; cook and stir 2 minutes. Add asparagus; cook and stir 5 minutes or until asparagus is crisp-tender. Season with pepper.

3. Transfer mixture to 2½-quart casserole. Top with stuffing mix.

4. Add wine to skillet, if desired; cook and stir over medium-high heat, scraping up any browned bits from bottom of skillet. Add broth and soup; cook and stir until well blended. Pour broth mixture over stuffing mix; mix well.

5. Bake 35 minutes or until heated through and lightly browned.

Makes 6 servings

Chicken & Dumplings Casserole

¾ pound chicken tenders, cut into bite-size pieces

6 baby red or Yukon Gold potatoes, quartered (about ½ pound)

1 cup baby carrots

1 cup frozen green peas, thawed

2 tablespoons all-purpose flour

   Salt and black pepper

1 can (about 14 ounces) chicken broth

½ cup biscuit baking mix

¼ cup water

1. Lightly coat microwavable 9-inch glass pie plate with nonstick cooking spray.

2. Place chicken, potatoes, carrots, peas, flour, salt and pepper in large resealable food storage bag. Seal bag and shake to coat chicken and vegetables with flour and seasonings. Pour chicken and vegetables evenly into prepared pie plate. Add broth. Cover with 10-inch circle of waxed paper and microwave on HIGH 20 minutes.

3. Preheat oven to 400°F.

4. Combine baking mix and water in small bowl; mix lightly with fork. Drop teaspoons of batter over chicken and vegetables.

5. Bake 10 minutes or until dumplings are puffed and cooked through. Let stand 5 minutes before serving.

Makes 6 servings

Chicken Ricotta Enchiladas

⅛ teaspoon garlic powder
⅛ teaspoon black pepper
1 pound chicken tenders
1 tablespoon olive oil
1 cup ricotta cheese
2 tablespoons finely chopped green onion
8 (6-inch) corn tortillas
¼ cup chicken broth
1 large tomato, chopped
½ cup chipotle salsa or other salsa
½ cup (2 ounces) shredded mozzarella cheese

1. Preheat oven to 450°F. Spray 13×9-inch baking dish with nonstick cooking spray.

2. Combine garlic powder and pepper in small bowl; sprinkle evenly over chicken. Heat oil in large nonstick skillet over medium-high heat. Add chicken; cook, without stirring, 4 minutes or until golden. Turn chicken; cook 4 minutes or until no longer pink in center.

3. Combine ricotta cheese and green onion in small bowl; mix well. Heat tortillas, one at a time, in medium skillet over medium heat 15 seconds per side.

4. Spread ricotta mixture across middle of warm tortillas; place chicken on top. Roll up tortillas; place seam side down in prepared baking dish. Drizzle broth evenly over top. Combine tomato and salsa in small bowl. Spoon over enchiladas; top with mozzarella cheese.

5. Bake, covered, 15 minutes or until heated through and cheese is melted.

Makes 4 servings

Chicken Ricotta Enchiladas

Chicken Veggie Casserole

1 can (10¾ ounces) condensed cheese soup, undiluted
1 cup milk
1½ cups chopped cooked chicken
1 can (about 16 ounces) sliced potatoes
1 can (about 15 ounces) mixed vegetables
2 cups biscuit baking mix
2 tablespoons mayonnaise
1 egg

1. Preheat oven to 400°F.

2. Bring soup and milk to a boil over medium-high heat in large saucepan, stirring constantly. Stir in chicken, potatoes and vegetables. Pour into 13×9-inch baking dish.

3. Combine baking mix, mayonnaise and egg in medium bowl; mix just until crumbly. Sprinkle over chicken mixture.

4. Bake 30 minutes or until browned and bubbly.   Makes 4 to 6 servings

Heartland Chicken Casserole

10 slices white bread, cubed
1½ cups cracker crumbs or dry bread crumbs, divided
4 cups cubed cooked chicken
3 cups chicken broth
1 cup *each* chopped onion and chopped celery
1 can (8 ounces) sliced mushrooms, drained
1 jar (about 4 ounces) pimientos, drained and diced
3 eggs, lightly beaten
   Salt and black pepper
1 tablespoon butter

1. Preheat oven to 350°F.

2. Combine bread cubes and 1 cup cracker crumbs in large bowl. Add chicken, broth, onion, celery, mushrooms, pimientos and eggs; mix well. Season with salt and pepper; spoon into 2½-quart casserole.

3. Melt butter in small saucepan over low heat. Add remaining ½ cup cracker crumbs; cook and stir until golden. Sprinkle crumbs over casserole.

4. Bake 1 hour or until hot and bubbly.   Makes 6 servings

Chicken Veggie Casserole

Chicken with Spinach and Artichokes

1 cup frozen chopped spinach, thawed and well drained
4 canned artichoke hearts, drained and chopped
¼ cup plus 2 tablespoons grated Parmesan cheese, divided
¼ cup chopped onion
¼ cup mayonnaise
½ teaspoon minced garlic
1 cup chopped cooked chicken

1. Preheat oven to 375°F. Coat 1-quart casserole with nonstick cooking spray.

2. Combine spinach, artichoke hearts, 2 tablespoons cheese, onion, mayonnaise and garlic in medium bowl. Place chicken in prepared casserole; top with spinach mixture and remaining ¼ cup cheese.

3. Bake 30 minutes or until cheese is browned.   Makes 2 servings

Hearty Chicken Bake

3 cups hot mashed potatoes
1 cup (4 ounces) shredded Cheddar cheese, divided
1⅓ cups FRENCH'S® French Fried Onions, divided
1½ cups (7 ounces) cubed cooked chicken
1 package (10 ounces) frozen mixed vegetables, thawed and drained
1 can (10¾ ounces) condensed cream of chicken soup
¼ cup milk
½ teaspoon ground mustard
¼ teaspoon garlic powder
¼ teaspoon pepper

1. Preheat oven to 375°F.

2. In medium bowl, combine mashed potatoes, ½ cup cheese and ⅔ *cup* French Fried Onions; mix thoroughly. Spoon potato mixture into greased 1½-quart casserole. Using back of spoon, spread potatoes across bottom and up sides of dish to form a shell. In large bowl, combine chicken, mixed vegetables, soup, milk and seasonings; pour into potato shell.

3. Bake, uncovered, 30 minutes or until heated through. Top with remaining ½ cup cheese and ⅔ *cup* onions. Bake, uncovered, 3 minutes or until onions are golden brown. Let stand 5 minutes before serving.   Makes 4 to 6 servings

Chicken with Spinach and Artichokes

Chicken & Biscuits

¼ cup (½ stick) butter
4 boneless skinless chicken breasts (about 1¼ pounds), cut into ½-inch pieces
½ cup chopped onion
½ teaspoon dried thyme
½ teaspoon paprika
¼ teaspoon black pepper
1 can (about 14 ounces) chicken broth, divided
⅓ cup all-purpose flour
1 package (10 ounces) frozen peas and carrots
1 can (12 ounces) refrigerated buttermilk biscuits

1. Preheat oven to 375°F.

2. Melt butter in large skillet over medium heat. Add chicken, onion, thyme, paprika and pepper; cook and stir 5 minutes or until chicken is browned.

3. Combine ¼ cup broth with flour in small bowl; stir until smooth. Add remaining broth to skillet; bring to a boil. Gradually add flour mixture, whisking constantly. Simmer 5 minutes. Add peas and carrots; cook 2 minutes. Transfer mixture to 1½-quart casserole; top with biscuits.

4. Bake 25 to 30 minutes or until biscuits are golden brown.

Makes 4 to 6 servings

tip

Regardless of the cooking method used, always cook chicken completely. Boneless chicken should be no longer pink in center; bone-in chicken should be 165°F. Do not partially cook it and then store it to finish cooking later.

Mom's Best Chicken Tetrazzini

8 ounces uncooked thin noodles or vermicelli pasta

2 tablespoons butter

8 ounces mushrooms, sliced

¼ cup chopped green onions

1 can (about 14 ounces) chicken broth

1 cup half-and-half, divided

2 tablespoons dry sherry

¼ cup all-purpose flour

½ teaspoon salt

¼ teaspoon ground nutmeg

⅛ teaspoon white pepper

1 jar (2 ounces) chopped pimientos, drained

½ cup grated Parmesan cheese, divided

½ cup sour cream

2 cups cubed cooked chicken

1. Preheat oven to 350°F. Spray 1½-quart casserole with nonstick cooking spray.

2. Cook noodles according to package directions; drain.

3. Meanwhile, melt butter in large nonstick skillet over medium-high heat. Add mushrooms and green onions; cook and stir until green onions are tender. Stir in broth, ½ cup half-and-half and sherry.

4. Pour remaining ½ cup half-and-half into small jar with tight-fitting lid; add flour, salt, nutmeg and pepper. Shake well. Slowly stir flour mixture into skillet. Bring to a boil; cook 1 minute. Reduce heat. Stir in pimientos, ¼ cup cheese and sour cream. Add noodles and chicken; mix well. Spread mixture evenly in prepared casserole. Sprinkle with remaining ¼ cup cheese.

5. Bake 30 to 35 minutes or until heated through.

Makes 6 servings

Mom's Best Chicken Tetrazzini

Artichoke-Olive Chicken Bake

1½ cups uncooked tri-colored rotini pasta
1 tablespoon olive oil
1 medium onion, chopped
½ green bell pepper, chopped
2 cups shredded cooked chicken
1 can (about 14 ounces) diced tomatoes with Italian herbs
1 can (14 ounces) artichoke hearts, drained and quartered
1 can (6 ounces) sliced black olives, drained
1 teaspoon Italian seasoning
2 cups (8 ounces) shredded mozzarella cheese

1. Preheat oven to 350°F. Spray 2-quart casserole with nonstick cooking spray. Cook pasta according to package directions; drain.

2. Heat oil in large skillet over medium heat. Add onion and bell pepper; cook and stir 1 minute. Add pasta, chicken, tomatoes, artichokes, olives and Italian seasoning; mix until blended. Place half of chicken mixture in prepared casserole; sprinkle with half of cheese. Top with remaining chicken mixture and cheese.

3. Bake, covered, 35 minutes or until hot and bubbly.   Makes 8 servings

Chicken in White Wine & Garlic Sauce Casserole

1 package TYSON® Heat 'N Eat Chicken Medallions in White Wine & Garlic Sauce*
1 cup cooked rice
1 package (10 ounces) frozen broccoli florets
1 package (10 ounces) frozen cut carrots
1 cup chicken broth

Look for TYSON® Heat 'N Eat Chicken Medallions in White Wine & Garlic Sauce in your supermarket's refrigerated meat case.

1. Preheat oven to 350°F. Place cooked rice in greased casserole dish. Evenly spread broccoli and carrots over rice. Pour chicken broth over vegetables and rice.

2. Remove clear wrap and sleeve from tray of chicken. Empty contents of bag onto rice and vegetables in casserole dish. Cover tightly with foil.

3. Bake in oven 20 to 25 minutes, until center is hot. Remove from oven and serve. Refrigerate leftovers immediately.   Makes 4 servings

Artichoke-Olive Chicken Bake

Spicy Chicken Casserole with Corn Bread

2 tablespoons olive oil

4 boneless skinless chicken breasts, cut into bite-size pieces

1 package (about 1 ounce) taco seasoning mix

1 can (about 15 ounces) black beans, rinsed and drained

1 can (about 14 ounces) diced tomatoes, drained

1 can (about 10 ounces) Mexican-style corn, drained

1 can (4 ounces) diced mild green chiles, drained

½ cup mild salsa

1 package (about 8 ounces) corn bread mix, plus ingredients to prepare mix

½ cup (2 ounces) shredded Cheddar cheese

¼ cup chopped red bell pepper

1. Preheat oven to 350°F. Spray 2-quart casserole with nonstick cooking spray.

2. Heat oil in large skillet over medium heat. Add chicken; cook and stir until cooked through.

3. Sprinkle taco seasoning over chicken. Add beans, tomatoes, corn, chiles and salsa; stir until well blended. Transfer to prepared casserole.

4. Prepare corn bread mix according to package directions, adding cheese and bell pepper. Spread batter over chicken mixture.

5. Bake 30 minutes or until corn bread is golden brown.   Makes 4 to 6 servings

Spicy Chicken Casserole with Corn Bread

Chicken & Rice Casserole

 2 cups cooked rice
 2 cups (8 ounces) shredded Monterey Jack cheese
 1½ cups cooked, chopped chicken breast meat
 1 can (12 fluid ounces) NESTLÉ® CARNATION® Evaporated Milk
 ½ cup finely chopped red onion
 2 large eggs, lightly beaten
 ¼ cup finely chopped cilantro
 2 tablespoons butter or margarine, melted
 1 tablespoon diced jalapeños

PREHEAT oven to 350°F. Lightly grease 2-quart casserole dish.

COMBINE rice, cheese, chicken, evaporated milk, onion, eggs, cilantro, butter and jalapeños in prepared casserole dish; stir well.

BAKE for 45 to 50 minutes or until knife inserted in center comes out clean. Season with salt.   Makes 6 servings

Prep Time: 15 minutes
Baking Time: 45 minutes

To Make Ahead and Freeze: Prepare as above; do not bake. Cover; freeze for up to 2 months. Thaw overnight in refrigerator. Uncover. Preheat oven to 350°F. Bake for 60 to 70 minutes or until knife inserted in center comes out clean. Season with salt.

Italian Chicken My Way

 ½ cup dry bread crumbs
 ¼ cup grated Parmesan cheese
 6 boneless skinless chicken breasts, cut in half lengthwise
 ¼ cup (½ stick) butter
 1 package (10 ounces) frozen chopped broccoli, thawed
 1 teaspoon garlic powder
 1 teaspoon Italian seasoning
 1 jar (26 ounces) pasta sauce
 2 cups (8 ounces) shredded mozzarella cheese

1. Preheat oven to 350°F. Spray 13×9-inch casserole with nonstick cooking spray.

2. Combine bread crumbs and Parmesan cheese in shallow bowl. Place chicken breast halves in bread crumb mixture, pressing to coat both sides.

3. Heat butter in large skillet over medium-high heat. Cook chicken in batches until browned on both sides. Transfer chicken to prepared casserole. Top with broccoli; sprinkle with garlic powder and Italian seasoning. Top with pasta sauce and mozzarella cheese.

4. Bake 25 minutes or until hot and bubbly and chicken is no longer pink in center.

Makes 12 servings

Chicken Vera Cruz

    1 chicken (3 pounds), cut up
    1 jar (12 ounces) salsa
  1⅓ cups FRENCH'S® French Fried Onions, divided
   ½ cup Spanish stuffed olives, sliced
   ½ cup beer or nonalcoholic malt beverage
   2 tablespoons lemon juice
   2 tablespoons chopped fresh parsley *or* 1 tablespoon dried parsley leaves
   ¼ teaspoon ground black pepper

1. Preheat oven to 350°F. Place chicken in 2-quart shallow dish. Bake, uncovered, 40 minutes. Drain.

2. Combine salsa, ⅔ *cup* French Fried Onions, olives, beer, lemon juice, parsley and pepper in medium saucepan. Bring to a boil. Reduce heat to low. Cook and stir 5 minutes or until slightly thickened. Pour sauce over chicken.

3. Bake 15 minutes or until chicken is no longer pink near bone. Sprinkle with remaining ⅔ *cup* onions. Bake 5 minutes or until onions are golden.

Makes 4 to 6 servings

Prep Time: 15 minutes
Bake Time: 60 minutes

Chicken Zucchini Casserole

1 package (about 6 ounces) herb-flavored stuffing mix
½ cup (1 stick) butter, melted
2 cups cubed zucchini, blanched and drained
1 can (14 ounces) condensed cream of celery soup, undiluted
1½ cups chopped cooked chicken
1 cup grated carrots
½ cup sour cream
1 onion, chopped
½ cup (2 ounces) shredded Cheddar cheese

1. Preheat oven to 350°F. Combine stuffing mix and butter in medium bowl; reserve 1 cup stuffing. Place remaining stuffing in 13×9-inch baking dish.

2. Combine zucchini, soup, chicken, carrots, sour cream and onion in large bowl. Pour mixture over stuffing in baking dish. Top with remaining 1 cup stuffing and cheese.

3. Bake 40 to 45 minutes or until heated through and cheese is melted.

Makes 8 servings

Chicken, Butternut Squash and Noodle Casserole

1 carton (18.3 ounces) CAMPBELL'S® V8® Butternut Squash Soup
1½ cups fresh or frozen peas, thawed
2 cups shredded cooked chicken breast
2 cups wide whole wheat egg noodles, cooked and drained
2 tablespoons bread crumbs
1 tablespoon olive oil

1. Stir the soup, peas, chicken and noodles in a 1½-quart casserole. Stir the bread crumbs and olive oil in a small bowl.

2. Bake at 400°F. for 20 minutes or until the chicken mixture is hot and bubbling. Stir the chicken mixture. Sprinkle with the bread crumb mixture.

3. Bake for 5 minutes or until the bread crumbs are golden brown.

Makes 4 servings

Prep Time: 20 minutes
Bake Time: 25 minutes

Chicken Zucchini Casserole

Broccoli Chicken Casserole

1 bag (22 ounces) TYSON® Grilled & Ready Frozen Fully Cooked
    Oven Roasted Diced Chicken Breasts
1 can (10¾ ounces) condensed cream of mushroom soup
½ cup milk
½ cup shredded Monterey Jack cheese
1 package (10 ounces) frozen broccoli
½ cup chopped green onion
1 teaspoon dried basil
½ teaspoon black pepper

1. Preheat oven to 375°F. Lightly grease 13×9-inch baking dish; set aside.

2. Combine chicken, soup, milk, cheese, broccoli, green onion, basil and pepper in large bowl; mix well. Spread in prepared baking dish. Bake 50 minutes, until bubbly. Refrigerate leftovers immediately.

Makes 6 servings

Prep Time: 10 minutes
Bake Time: 50 minutes

Creamy Chicken Success

1 bag SUCCESS® White Rice
    Non-stick cooking spray
1½ cups fat free sour cream
1 can (4 ounces) chopped green chilies, drained
1 cup (4 ounces) shredded Monterey Jack cheese
1 cup (4 ounces) shredded low-fat cheddar cheese
1 tablespoon olive oil
4 boneless skinless chicken breasts, cut into strips
1 tablespoon Worcestershire sauce

Preheat oven to 375°F. Prepare rice according to package directions.

Spray 1½-quart casserole dish with cooking spray; set aside. Combine sour cream and chilies in small bowl; set aside. Combine cheeses in separate small bowl.

Heat oil in large skillet over medium heat. Add chicken; cook and stir until no longer pink in center. Stir in Worcestershire sauce. Place chicken breasts in prepared casserole; cover with layers of rice, sour cream mixture and cheese mixture. Bake until cheese is melted, about 15 minutes.

Makes 4 servings

Broccoli Chicken Casserole

Sunday Dinner Casserole

2 cups egg noodles, cooked and drained
2 pounds boneless skinless chicken breasts
2 cups sliced sweet onions
½ cup dry sherry
2 tablespoons sugar
2 tablespoons balsamic vinegar
1 teaspoon dried thyme
½ teaspoon black pepper
3 cups chicken broth
1 can (about 14 ounces) diced tomatoes, drained
2 cloves garlic, minced
½ teaspoon red pepper flakes
¼ cup chopped fresh basil
2 teaspoons grated lemon peel

1. Preheat oven to 400°F.

2. Place noodles in 13×9-inch baking dish. Top with chicken.

3. Combine onions, sherry, sugar, vinegar, thyme and black pepper in large skillet; cook and stir over medium heat until onions begin to brown.

4. Add broth, tomatoes, garlic and red pepper flakes to onion mixture in skillet; pour over chicken.

5. Bake 20 minutes. Turn chicken; bake 20 to 25 minutes or until chicken is no longer pink in center. Sprinkle with basil and lemon peel.   Makes 4 to 6 servings

Sunday Dinner Casserole

Chicken Tetrazzini

8 ounces uncooked vermicelli pasta, broken in half

1 can (10¾ ounces) condensed cream of mushroom soup, undiluted

¼ cup half-and-half

3 tablespoons dry sherry

½ teaspoon salt

⅛ to ¼ teaspoon red pepper flakes

2 cups chopped cooked chicken

1 cup frozen peas

½ cup grated Parmesan cheese

1 cup coarse fresh bread crumbs

2 tablespoons butter, melted

   Chopped fresh basil (optional)

1. Preheat oven to 375°F. Spray 8-inch square baking dish with nonstick cooking spray.

2. Cook pasta according to package directions; drain.

3. Meanwhile, combine soup, half-and-half, sherry, salt and red pepper flakes in large bowl. Stir in chicken, peas and cheese. Add pasta; stir until well coated. Pour into prepared dish. Combine bread crumbs and butter in small bowl. Sprinkle evenly over casserole.

4. Bake 25 to 30 minutes or until heated through and crumbs are golden brown. Sprinkle with basil, if desired.   Makes 4 servings

Chicken Tetrazzini

Barbecue Chicken with Corn Bread Topper

1½ pounds boneless skinless chicken breasts and thighs, cut into ¾-inch cubes

1 can (about 15 ounces) red beans, rinsed and drained

1 can (8 ounces) tomato sauce

1 cup chopped green bell pepper

½ cup barbecue sauce

1 package (6 ounces) corn bread mix, plus ingredients to prepare mix

1. Preheat oven to 375°F.

2. Heat large nonstick skillet over medium heat. Add chicken; cook and stir 5 minutes or until cooked through.

3. Combine chicken, beans, tomato sauce, bell pepper and barbecue sauce in microwavable 8-inch baking dish. Loosely cover chicken mixture with plastic wrap or waxed paper. Microwave on MEDIUM-HIGH (70%) 8 minutes or until heated through, stirring after 4 minutes.

4. Meanwhile, prepare corn bread mix according to package directions. Spoon batter over chicken mixture.

5. Bake 15 to 18 minutes or until toothpick inserted into center of corn bread layer comes out clean.   Makes 8 servings

tip

Many microwaves have "hot spots" or areas where food cooks more quickly. Rotating food helps solve the problem of uneven cooking because of hot spots. If your microwave does not have a carousel, rotate the dish a quarter or a half turn at even intervals during cooking. Be sure to rotate the dish in the same direction each time.

Barbecue Chicken with Corn Bread Topper

Creamy Chicken and Pasta with Spinach

6 ounces uncooked egg noodles

1 tablespoon olive oil

¼ cup chopped onion

¼ cup chopped red bell pepper

2 boneless skinless chicken breasts (¾ pound), cooked and cut into 1-inch pieces

1 package (10 ounces) frozen chopped spinach, thawed and drained

1 can (4 ounces) sliced mushrooms, drained

2 cups (8 ounces) shredded Swiss cheese

1 container (8 ounces) sour cream

¾ cup half-and-half

2 eggs, lightly beaten

½ teaspoon salt

1. Preheat oven to 350°F. Spray 13×9-inch baking dish with nonstick cooking spray.

2. Cook noodles according to package directions; drain.

3. Heat oil in large skillet over medium-high heat. Add onion and bell pepper; cook and stir 2 minutes or until onion is tender. Add noodles, chicken, spinach and mushrooms; stir to blend.

4. Combine cheese, sour cream, half-and-half, eggs and salt in medium bowl; blend well. Add cheese mixture to chicken mixture; stir to blend. Transfer to prepared baking dish.

5. Bake, covered, 30 to 35 minutes or until heated through.   Makes 8 servings

Serving Suggestion: Serve with orange slices sprinkled with coconut.

Creamy Chicken and Pasta with Spinach

Biscuit-Topped Chicken Pot Pie

1½ pounds boneless skinless chicken breasts, cut into 1-inch chunks
¼ cup chicken broth
1 bag (16 ounces) frozen mixed vegetables, such as cauliflower, carrots, broccoli, zucchini and red bell pepper
1 can (10¾ ounces) condensed cream of chicken soup, undiluted
4 tablespoons grated Parmesan cheese, divided
1 teaspoon dried thyme
½ teaspoon black pepper
1½ cups biscuit baking mix
½ cup milk

1. Preheat oven to 400°F. Combine chicken and broth in large saucepan; bring to a boil over high heat. Reduce heat; simmer 8 minutes or until chicken is cooked through, stirring occasionally. Stir in vegetables, soup, 2 tablespoons cheese, thyme and pepper; mix well. Cook until heated through. Transfer mixture to 8-inch square baking dish.

2. Combine baking mix and milk in small bowl; mix just until dry ingredients are moistened. Drop batter by heaping tablespoonfuls over hot chicken mixture; top with remaining 2 tablespoons cheese.

3. Bake 14 to 16 minutes or until bubbly and biscuits are golden brown.

Makes 6 servings

Herbed Chicken and Potatoes

2 medium all-purpose potatoes, thinly sliced (about 1 pound)
8 lemon slices (optional)
4 bone-in chicken breast halves (about 2 pounds)*
1 envelope LIPTON® RECIPE SECRETS® Savory Herb with Garlic Soup Mix
⅓ cup water
1 tablespoon olive oil

Substitution: Use 1 (2½- to 3-pound) chicken, cut into serving pieces.

1. Preheat oven to 375°F. In 13×9-inch baking or roasting pan, combine potatoes and lemon; arrange chicken on top.

2. Pour soup mix blended with water and oil over chicken and potatoes.

3. Bake 50 minutes or until chicken is thoroughly cooked and potatoes are tender.

Makes 4 servings

Biscuit-Topped Chicken Pot Pie

Crunchy Top & Flaky Bottom Broccoli Casserole

2 cans (8 ounces each) refrigerated crescent roll dough

1 package (16 ounces) frozen chopped broccoli

2 cups (8 ounces) shredded mozzarella cheese, divided

1½ cups French fried onions, coarsely crushed and divided

1 can (10¾ ounces) condensed cream of mushroom soup, undiluted

10 ounces thinly sliced ham, cut into bite-size pieces

½ cup mayonnaise

2 eggs, beaten

2 tablespoons Dijon mustard

1 tablespoon prepared horseradish

1 jar (2 ounces) chopped pimientos, drained

1 teaspoon finely chopped fresh parsley

1. Preheat oven to 375°F. Grease bottom of 13×9-inch baking dish.

2. Unroll dough; do not separate. Press dough onto bottom of prepared baking dish, sealing all seams.

3. Bake 7 minutes.

4. Combine broccoli, 1 cup cheese, ½ cup onions, soup, ham, mayonnaise, eggs, mustard and horseradish in large bowl. Spread evenly over crust. Top with remaining 1 cup onions, 1 cup cheese, pimientos and parsley.

5. Bake 20 to 25 minutes or until set. Let stand 10 minutes before serving.

Makes 8 servings

Pork and Corn Bread Stuffing Casserole

½ teaspoon paprika

¼ teaspoon salt

¼ teaspoon garlic powder

¼ teaspoon black pepper

4 bone-in pork chops (about 1¾ pounds)

2 tablespoons butter

1½ cups chopped onions

¾ cup thinly sliced celery

¾ cup matchstick carrots*

¼ cup chopped fresh Italian parsley

1 can (about 14 ounces) chicken broth

4 cups corn bread stuffing mix

Matchstick carrots (sometimes called shredded carrots) can be found near other prepared vegetables in the supermarket produce section.

1. Preheat oven to 350°F. Lightly coat 13×9-inch baking dish with nonstick cooking spray.

2. Combine paprika, salt, garlic powder and pepper in small bowl; sprinkle over both sides of pork chops.

3. Melt butter in large skillet over medium-high heat. Add pork chops; cook 4 minutes or just until browned, turning once. Transfer to plate.

4. Add onions, celery, carrots and parsley to same skillet; cook and stir 4 minutes or until onions are translucent. Add broth; bring to a boil. Remove from heat. Add stuffing mix and fluff with fork. Transfer stuffing mixture to prepared baking dish. Top with pork chops.

5. Bake, covered, 25 minutes or until pork is barely pink in center.

Makes 4 servings

Pork and Corn Bread Stuffing Casserole

Ham, Poblano and Potato Casserole

¼ cup (½ stick) butter

¼ cup all-purpose flour

1½ cups whole milk

2 pounds baking potatoes, halved and thinly sliced

6 ounces thinly sliced ham, cut into bite-size pieces

1 poblano pepper, cut into thin strips (about 1 cup)

1 cup corn

1 cup chopped red bell pepper

1 cup finely chopped onion

Salt and black pepper

¼ teaspoon ground nutmeg

1½ cups (6 ounces) shredded sharp Cheddar cheese

1. Preheat oven to 350°F. Lightly coat 13×9-inch baking dish with nonstick cooking spray.

2. Melt butter in medium saucepan over medium heat. Add flour; whisk until smooth. Add milk; whisk until smooth. Cook and stir 5 to 7 minutes or until thickened. Remove from heat.

3. Layer one third of potatoes, half of ham, poblano pepper, corn, bell pepper and onion in prepared baking dish. Sprinkle with salt, black pepper and nutmeg. Repeat layers. Top with remaining one third of potatoes. Spoon white sauce evenly over potatoes.

4. Bake, covered, 45 minutes. Bake, uncovered, 30 minutes or until potatoes are tender. Sprinkle with cheese. Bake 5 minutes or until cheese is melted. Let stand 15 minutes before serving.

Makes 6 servings

tip

To make this casserole even easier, use a food processor with the slicing blade attachment to thinly slice the potatoes.

Ham, Poblano and Potato Casserole

Wisconsin Swiss Ham and Noodles Casserole

   2 tablespoons butter

½ cup chopped onion

½ cup chopped green bell pepper

   1 can (10½ ounces) condensed cream of mushroom soup

   1 cup dairy sour cream

   1 package (8 ounces) medium noodles, cooked and drained

   2 cups (8 ounces) shredded Wisconsin Swiss cheese

   2 cups cubed cooked ham (about ¾ pound)

In 1-quart saucepan, melt butter; sauté onion and bell pepper. Remove from heat; stir in soup and sour cream. In buttered 2-quart casserole, layer ⅓ of the noodles, ⅓ of the Swiss cheese, ⅓ of the ham and ½ of the soup mixture. Repeat layers, ending with final ⅓ layer of the noodles, cheese and ham. Bake in preheated 350°F oven 30 to 45 minutes or until heated through.   Makes 6 to 8 servings

Favorite recipe from **Wisconsin Milk Marketing Board**

Pork with Savory Apple Stuffing

   1 package (6 ounces) corn bread stuffing mix

   1 can (14½ ounces) chicken broth

   1 small apple, peeled, cored and chopped

¼ cup chopped celery

1⅓ cups FRENCH'S® French Fried Onions, divided

   4 boneless pork chops, ¾ inch thick (about 1 pound)

½ cup peach-apricot sweet & sour sauce

   1 tablespoon FRENCH'S® Honey Dijon Mustard

1. Preheat oven to 375°F. Combine stuffing mix, broth, apple, celery and ⅔ *cup* French Fried Onions in large bowl. Spoon into bottom of greased shallow 2-quart baking dish. Arrange pork chops on top of stuffing.

2. Combine sweet & sour sauce with mustard in small bowl. Pour over pork. Bake 40 minutes or until pork is no longer pink in center.

3. Sprinkle with remaining ⅔ *cup* onions. Bake 5 minutes or until onions are golden.

Makes 4 servings

Wisconsin Swiss Ham and Noodles Casserole

Glazed Pork Chops with Corn Stuffing

1¾ cups SWANSON® Chicken Stock

⅛ teaspoon ground red pepper

1 cup frozen whole kernel corn

1 stalk celery, chopped (about ½ cup)

1 medium onion, chopped (about ½ cup)

4 cups PEPPERIDGE FARM® Corn Bread Stuffing

Vegetable cooking spray

6 boneless pork chops, ¾-inch thick (about 1½ pounds)

2 tablespoons packed brown sugar

2 teaspoons spicy-brown mustard

1. Heat the stock, red pepper, corn, celery and onion in a 3-quart saucepan over medium heat to a boil. Remove the saucepan from the heat. Add the stuffing and mix lightly.

2. Spray a 3-quart shallow baking dish with the cooking spray. Spoon the stuffing into the baking dish. Top with the pork. Stir the brown sugar and mustard in a small bowl until the mixture is smooth. Spread the brown sugar mixture over the pork.

3. Bake at 400°F. for 30 minutes or until the pork is cooked through.

Makes 6 servings

Prep Time: 15 minutes
Bake Time: 30 minutes
Total Time: 45 minutes

Glazed Pork Chops with Corn Stuffing

Cassoulet

Bretonne* (page 154)
5 slices bacon
1 pound smoked sausage, cut into ¼-inch slices
1 boneless pork loin roast (about ¾ pound), cut into 1-inch cubes
½ cup water
2 tablespoons packed brown sugar
1 tablespoon lemon juice
Fresh oregano sprigs (optional)

*Bretonne is the classic French name for a dish of seasoned beans.

1. Prepare Bretonne.

2. Preheat oven to 350°F. Grease 2½-quart casserole or Dutch oven.

3. Cook bacon in large skillet over medium-high heat until crisp, turning occasionally. Drain bacon on paper towels, reserving 2 tablespoons drippings in skillet. Crumble bacon; set aside.

4. Add one quarter of sausage and pork to reserved drippings in skillet; cook until browned on all sides. Remove sausage and pork to paper towels; drain well. Repeat with remaining sausage and pork; set aside.

5. Pour off and discard drippings. Pour water into skillet; cook over medium-high heat 2 minutes, stirring to scrape up browned bits. Stir in brown sugar and lemon juice; bring to a boil. Boil 1 minute. Stir sugar mixture and crumbled bacon into Bretonne.

6. Spread half of Bretonne in prepared casserole. Top with browned sausage and pork. Spoon remaining Bretonne over top.

7. Bake, covered, 2 hours. Let stand 10 minutes before serving. Garnish with oregano.

Makes 8 servings

continued on page 154

Cassoulet, continued

Bretonne

  1 pound dried Great Northern beans
  2 tablespoons butter
  2 cups chopped onions
  2 cloves garlic, minced
  1 can (about 14 ounces) diced tomatoes
½ cup red wine
  2 tablespoons chopped fresh parsley
  2 tablespoons chopped fresh basil
  2 tablespoons chopped fresh thyme
    Salt and black pepper
  4 cups water
  1 large carrot, cut into 2-inch pieces
  1 large onion, halved
  2 large sprigs *each* fresh parsley, basil, thyme and oregano

1. Rinse beans thoroughly in colander under cold running water, picking out debris and any blemished beans. Place beans in large bowl; add water to cover by 3 inches. Cover; let stand at room temperature overnight.

2. Meanwhile, melt butter in large saucepan over medium-high heat. Add chopped onions and garlic; cook and stir 8 to 10 minutes or until onions are softened. Stir in tomatoes, wine, parsley, basil, thyme, salt and pepper; bring to a boil. Reduce heat to low; simmer, uncovered, 20 minutes or until mixture is reduced to 2¼ cups. Transfer mixture to small bowl; cover and refrigerate overnight.

3. Drain beans; discard soaking water. Combine beans, 4 cups water, carrot, halved onion and herb sprigs in large saucepan or Dutch oven; bring to a boil over high heat. Reduce heat to low; partially cover and simmer 1 hour or until beans are tender but firm.

4. Remove beans to large bowl with slotted spoon, leaving cooking liquid in saucepan. Remove and discard carrot, halved onion and herb sprigs.

5. Bring cooking liquid to a boil over high heat. Reduce heat to medium; cook until liquid is reduced to ½ cup. Add liquid to beans. Stir tomato mixture into beans until blended.

Makes about 6 cups

Pork-Stuffed Peppers

1 pound ground pork
3 large green peppers
¼ cup raisins
⅓ cup chopped onion
½ cup chopped carrot
½ cup chopped celery
¼ teaspoon salt
1 cup cooked brown rice
2 tablespoons sunflower kernels
½ cup plain yogurt

Remove tops, seeds and membranes from peppers. Cut in half lengthwise. Cook in boiling salted water 5 minutes; drain.

Soak raisins in water 10 to 15 minutes; drain and set aside. Combine pork, onion, carrot, celery and salt in medium skillet. Cook over low heat until pork is done and vegetables are tender, stirring occasionally. Drain thoroughly. Add rice, sunflower kernels, yogurt and raisins; mix well. Spoon mixture into peppers. Place in 12×8×2-inch baking dish. Bake at 350°F 30 to 35 minutes or until heated through.

Makes 6 servings

Prep Time: 20 minutes
Bake Time: 30 minutes

Favorite recipe from **National Pork Board**

Hurry-Up Lasagna

1 jar (48 ounces) tomato and sliced mushroom pasta sauce
2 packages (9 ounces each) fresh fettuccine, uncooked
4 cups (30 ounces) SARGENTO® Whole Milk Ricotta Cheese
1 cup minced fresh parsley
4 ounces thinly sliced pepperoni, divided
3 cups (12 ounces) SARGENTO® Fancy Shredded Pizza Double Cheese®, divided

1. Spread 1 cup sauce in bottom of 13×9-inch baking pan. Carefully place one-third uncooked fettuccine over sauce, making sure fettuccine is covered with sauce.

2. Combine Ricotta cheese and parsley. Layer 2 cups Ricotta mixture, half of the pepperoni, 1 cup sauce and 1 cup shredded cheese. Repeat layers of fettuccine, 2 cups Ricotta mixture, pepperoni, sauce and 1 cup shredded cheese. Top with remaining fettuccine and sauce, making sure sauce completely covers fettuccine.

3. Cover and bake in preheated 375°F oven 1 hour. Uncover; bake 5 minutes more. Sprinkle with remaining 1 cup shredded cheese. Let stand 10 minutes before serving. Makes 10 servings

Prep Time: 20 minutes
Bake Time: 65 minutes

Potato and Pork Frittata

12 ounces (about 3 cups) frozen hash brown potatoes

  1 teaspoon Cajun seasoning

  4 egg whites

  2 eggs

¼ cup milk

  1 teaspoon dry mustard

¼ teaspoon black pepper

10 ounces (about 3 cups) frozen stir-fry vegetable blend

⅓ cup water

¾ cup chopped cooked pork

½ cup (2 ounces) shredded Cheddar cheese

1. Preheat oven to 400°F. Spray baking sheet with nonstick cooking spray.

2. Spread potatoes on prepared baking sheet; sprinkle with Cajun seasoning.

3. Bake 15 minutes or until heated through. Remove from oven. *Reduce oven temperature to 350°F.*

4. Beat egg whites, eggs, milk, mustard and pepper in small bowl. Place vegetables and water in medium ovenproof nonstick skillet; cook over medium heat 5 minutes or until vegetables are tender. Drain.

5. Add potatoes and pork to vegetables in skillet; stir lightly. Add egg mixture; sprinkle with cheese. Cook over medium-low heat 5 minutes.

6. Bake 5 minutes or until egg mixture is set and cheese is melted.

Makes 4 servings

Potato and Pork Frittata

Spicy Pork Chop Casserole

1 tablespoon plus 1 teaspoon olive oil, divided

2 cups frozen corn

2 cups frozen diced potatoes

1 can (about 14 ounces) diced tomatoes with basil, garlic and oregano, drained

2 teaspoons chili powder

1 teaspoon dried oregano

½ teaspoon ground cumin

⅛ teaspoon red pepper flakes

4 boneless pork loin chops (about 3 ounces each), cut about ¾ inch thick

¼ teaspoon black pepper

¼ cup (1 ounce) shredded Monterey Jack cheese (optional)

1. Preheat oven to 375°F. Spray 8-inch square baking dish with nonstick cooking spray.

2. Heat 1 tablespoon oil in large nonstick skillet over medium-high heat. Add corn; cook and stir 5 minutes or until corn begins to brown. Add potatoes; cook and stir 5 minutes or until potatoes begin to brown. Add tomatoes, chili powder, oregano, cumin and red pepper flakes; stir until blended. Transfer to prepared dish.

3. Wipe out skillet with paper towel. Heat remaining 1 teaspoon oil in skillet over medium-high heat. Add pork; cook until browned on one side. Place browned side up on top of corn mixture. Sprinkle with black pepper.

4. Bake 20 minutes or until pork is barely pink in center. Sprinkle with cheese, if desired. Let stand 5 minutes before serving. Makes 4 servings

Spicy Pork Chop Casserole

Macaroni & Cheese with Bacon & Tomatoes

4 thick slices applewood smoked bacon, diced
2 tablespoons all-purpose flour
2¼ cups milk
½ teaspoon salt
⅛ teaspoon cayenne pepper
1¾ cups (7 ounces) SARGENTO® Shredded Colby-Jack Cheese, divided
8 ounces (2 cups dry) multi-grain or regular elbow macaroni, cooked and drained
1 can (14 ounces) fire-roasted diced tomatoes, drained

1. Cook bacon in a large saucepan over medium heat 5 to 6 minutes or until crisp, stirring frequently. Use a slotted spoon to transfer bacon to a paper towel; set aside.

2. Add flour to drippings in pan; cook and stir 30 seconds. Add milk, salt and cayenne pepper; bring to a boil. Simmer 1 minute or until sauce thickens, stirring frequently. Remove from heat; stir in 1¼ cups cheese until melted. Stir in cooked macaroni and tomatoes. Transfer to a sprayed 9-inch baking dish or shallow 1½-quart casserole.

3. Bake in a preheated 375°F oven 20 minutes or until heated through. Sprinkle reserved bacon and remaining cheese over macaroni. Continue to bake 5 minutes or until cheese is melted.

Makes 6 servings

Prep Time: 15 minutes
Bake Time: 25 minutes

Carolina Baked Beans & Pork Chops

2 cans (16 ounces each) pork and beans
½ cup chopped onion
½ cup chopped green bell pepper
¼ cup FRENCH'S® Classic Yellow® Mustard
¼ cup packed light brown sugar
2 tablespoons FRENCH'S® Worcestershire Sauce
1 tablespoon FRANK'S® REDHOT® Original Cayenne Pepper Sauce
6 boneless pork chops (1 inch thick)

1. Preheat oven to 400°F. Combine all ingredients *except pork chops* in 3-quart shallow baking dish; mix well. Arrange pork chops on top, turning once to coat with sauce.

2. Bake, uncovered, 30 to 35 minutes or until pork is no longer pink in center. Stir beans around chops once during baking. Serve with green beans or mashed potatoes, if desired.

Makes 6 servings

Prep Time: 10 minutes
Bake Time: 30 minutes

Peppered Pork & Pilaf

1 large size (14×20-inch) oven cooking bag
2 tablespoons all-purpose flour
1 pound ALWAYS TENDER® peppercorn flavored pork tenderloin
2 medium green, red and/or yellow bell peppers, cut into thin strips
1 small red onion, cut into thin wedges
1 cup uncooked instant white rice
1 (1.2-ounce) brown gravy mix
2 teaspoons HERB-OX® sodium free beef flavored bouillon
3 cups water

Preheat oven to 350°F. Add flour to oven bag; twist end of bag and shake to coat with flour. Place oven bag into a 13×9-inch baking dish. Add pork, peppers, onion, rice, gravy mix, bouillon and water. Gently squeeze bag to blend ingredients. Arrange ingredients in an even layer in pan. Cut six (½-inch) slits in the top of the bag. Bake 40 minutes or until the pork is cooked through.

Makes 4 servings

Carolina Baked Beans & Pork Chop

Baked Pasta and Cheese Supreme

8 ounces uncooked fusilli pasta or other corkscrew-shaped pasta

12 slices bacon, diced

½ medium onion, chopped

2 cloves garlic, minced

2 teaspoons dried oregano, divided

1 can (8 ounces) tomato sauce

1 teaspoon hot pepper sauce (optional)

1½ cups (6 ounces) shredded Cheddar or Colby cheese

½ cup fresh bread crumbs (from 1 slice of white bread)

1 tablespoon butter, melted

1. Preheat oven to 400°F.

2. Cook pasta according to package directions; drain.

3. Meanwhile, cook bacon in large ovenproof skillet over medium heat until crisp. Drain on paper towels; set aside. Add onion, garlic and 1 teaspoon oregano to skillet; cook and stir 3 minutes or until onion is translucent. Stir in tomato sauce and hot pepper sauce, if desired. Add pasta and cheese; stir to coat.

4. Combine bacon, bread crumbs, remaining 1 teaspoon oregano and butter in small bowl; sprinkle over pasta mixture.

5. Bake 15 minutes or until hot and bubbly. Makes 4 servings

tip

To chop onions, first peel the skin. Cut in half through the root end with a utility knife. Place one onion half, cut side down, on a cutting board. Cut the onion into slices perpendicular to the root end, holding the onion with your fingers to keep it together. Turn the onion half and cut it crosswise.

Baked Pasta and Cheese Supreme

Old-Fashioned Cabbage Rolls

8 ounces ground beef
8 ounces ground veal
8 ounces ground pork
1 small onion, chopped
2 eggs, lightly beaten
½ cup plain dry bread crumbs
1 teaspoon salt
1 teaspoon molasses
¼ teaspoon ground ginger
¼ teaspoon ground nutmeg
¼ teaspoon ground allspice
1 large head cabbage, separated into leaves
3 cups boiling water
¼ cup (½ stick) butter
½ cup milk, plus additional if necessary
1 tablespoon cornstarch

1. Combine beef, veal, pork and onion in large bowl. Combine eggs, bread crumbs, salt, molasses, ginger, nutmeg and allspice in medium bowl; mix well. Add to meat mixture; stir until well blended.

2. Drop cabbage leaves into boiling water 3 minutes. Remove with slotted spoon; reserve ½ cup boiling liquid.

3. Preheat oven to 375°F.

4. Place about 2 tablespoons meat mixture about 1 inch from stem end of each cabbage leaf. Fold sides in and roll up, fastening with toothpicks, if necessary.

5. Heat butter in large skillet over medium-high heat. Add cabbage rolls, 3 or 4 at a time; brown on all sides. Arrange rolls, seam side down, in single layer in 3-quart casserole. Combine reserved boiling liquid with butter remaining in skillet; pour over cabbage rolls.

6. Bake 1 hour. Carefully drain accumulated pan juices into measuring cup. Return cabbage rolls to oven.

7. Add enough milk to pan juices to equal 1 cup. Pour milk mixture into small saucepan. Stir in cornstarch; bring to a boil, stirring constantly until sauce is thickened. Pour over cabbage rolls.

8. Bake 15 minutes or until cabbage is tender and sauce begins to bubble.

Makes 8 servings

Old-Fashioned Cabbage Rolls

Savory Lentil Casserole

1¼ cups dried brown or green lentils, sorted and rinsed

2 tablespoons olive oil

1 large onion, chopped

3 cloves garlic, minced

8 ounces fresh shiitake or button mushrooms, sliced

2 tablespoons all-purpose flour

1½ cups beef broth

4 ounces Canadian bacon, minced

1 tablespoon Worcestershire sauce

1 tablespoon balsamic vinegar

Salt and black pepper

½ cup grated Parmesan cheese

2 to 3 plum tomatoes, seeded and chopped

Fresh Italian parsley (optional)

1. Preheat oven to 400°F. Grease 1½-quart casserole.

2. Place lentils in medium saucepan; add water to cover by 1-inch. Bring to a boil over high heat. Reduce heat to low. Simmer, covered, 20 to 25 minutes or until lentils are just tender; drain.

3. Meanwhile, heat oil in large skillet over medium heat. Add onion and garlic; cook and stir 5 minutes. Add mushrooms; cook and stir 10 minutes or until liquid is evaporated and mushrooms are tender. Sprinkle flour over mushroom mixture; cook and stir 1 minute. Stir in broth, Canadian bacon, Worcestershire sauce, vinegar, salt and pepper; cook and stir until mixture is thick and bubbly.

4. Stir lentils into mushroom mixture. Spread evenly in prepared casserole. Sprinkle with cheese.

5. Bake 20 minutes. Sprinkle tomatoes over casserole just before serving. Garnish with parsley.

Makes 4 servings

Savory Lentil Casserole

Ham Asparagus Gratin

1 can (10¾ ounces) CAMPBELL'S® Condensed Cream of Asparagus Soup
½ cup milk
¼ teaspoon onion powder
¼ teaspoon ground black pepper
1½ cups cooked cut asparagus
1½ cups cubed cooked ham
2¼ cups corkscrew-shaped pasta (rotini), cooked and drained
1 cup shredded Cheddar cheese or Swiss cheese

1. Stir the soup, milk, onion powder, black pepper, asparagus, ham, pasta and ½ cup cheese in a 2-quart shallow baking dish.

2. Bake at 400°F. for 25 minutes or until the ham mixture is hot and bubbling. Stir the ham mixture. Sprinkle with the remaining cheese.

3. Bake for 5 minutes or until the cheese is melted.   Makes 4 servings

Prep Time: 20 minutes
Bake Time: 30 minutes
Total Time: 50 minutes

Harvest Pot Roast

1 large size (14×20-inch) oven cooking bag
¼ cup all-purpose flour
1 (2½- to 3-pound) ALWAYS TENDER® boneless pork roast
1 pound medium-size new red potatoes, quartered
1 large onion, cut into thin wedges
1 cup baby carrots, cut in half
2 stalks celery, cut diagonally into 1-inch pieces
1 cup vegetable juice
1 tablespoon HERB-OX® reduced sodium beef flavored bouillon
1 clove garlic, minced
1 bay leaf

Preheat oven to 350°F. Add flour to oven bag; twist end of bag and shake to coat. Place oven bag into 13×9-inch baking dish. Add pork and remaining ingredients. Gently squeeze bag to blend ingredients. Close bag and secure with twist tie. Cut six (½-inch) slits in top of bag. Bake 2 to 2½ hours or until pork has reached an internal temperature of 160°F and vegetables are fork-tender.   Makes 6 servings

Ham Asparagus Gratin

Zippy Pork Bake

8 ounces fusilli pasta or other small pasta
1 tablespoon butter
1 teaspoon minced garlic
1 pound ground pork
2 medium zucchini, thinly sliced
1 cup fresh sliced mushrooms
2 tablespoons sliced green onions
1½ teaspoons chili powder
1 teaspoon salt
4 ounce can chopped green chilies
½ cup sour cream
1 cup shredded mozzarella cheese, divided
Browned bread crumbs (optional)
Chopped parsley for garnish

Cook pasta according to package directions; drain.

In large skillet over medium-high heat, melt butter; add garlic and sauté until slightly brown. Add pork and cook until no longer pink, about 6 minutes. Add zucchini, mushrooms and onions; cook and stir until tender. Drain.

Stir in chili powder and salt. Add chilies, sour cream, pasta and ½ cup cheese. Pour into 2½-quart baking dish coated with nonstick spray. Top with remaining cheese and bread crumbs, if desired. Bake, uncovered, in preheated 350°F oven for 20 minutes or until cheese is melted. Garnish with parsley.   Makes 6 servings

Note: Can be made in advance and refrigerated. Bake until heated through.

Favorite recipe from **North Dakota Wheat Commission**

Pork-Stuffed Eggplant

½ pound lean ground pork
1 medium eggplant
1 small green pepper, coarsely chopped
¼ cup chopped onion
1 clove garlic, minced
¼ cup water
⅛ teaspoon dried oregano leaves, crushed
⅛ teaspoon ground black pepper
1 medium tomato, coarsely chopped

Wash eggplant and cut in half lengthwise. Remove pulp, leaving eggplant shell about ¼ inch thick. Cut pulp into ½-inch cubes. Set shells and pulp aside.

In large skillet cook ground pork, green pepper, onion and garlic until pork is browned; drain excess drippings. Add eggplant pulp, water, oregano and black pepper; cover and cook over low heat 10 minutes, stirring occasionally. Remove from heat and stir in tomato. Spoon mixture into eggplant shells. Place in 12×8×2-inch baking dish. Bake in 350°F oven 20 to 25 minutes or until heated through.   Makes 2 servings

Prep Time: 25 minutes
Bake Time: 25 minutes

Favorite recipe from **National Pork Board**

Macaroni & Cheese with Bacon

> 8 ounces uncooked rotini pasta
> 2 tablespoons butter
> 2 tablespoons all-purpose flour
> ¼ teaspoon salt
> ¼ teaspoon dry mustard
> ⅛ teaspoon black pepper
> 1½ cups milk
> 2 cups (8 ounces) shredded sharp Cheddar cheese
> 12 slices bacon, crisp-cooked and crumbled*
> 2 medium tomatoes, sliced

*You may substitute 1 cup cubed cooked ham for the bacon.

1. Preheat oven to 350°F. Lightly grease shallow 1½-quart casserole.

2. Cook pasta according to package directions; drain.

3. Melt butter in large saucepan over medium-low heat. Whisk in flour, salt, mustard and pepper; cook and stir 1 minute. Whisk in milk; bring to a boil over medium heat, stirring frequently. Reduce heat and simmer 2 minutes. Remove from heat. Add cheese; stir until melted. Add cheese mixture and bacon to pasta; stir until well blended. Transfer to prepared casserole.

4. Bake 20 minutes. Arrange tomato slices on casserole. Bake 5 to 8 minutes or until hot and bubbly.   Makes 4 servings

Harvest Casserole

1 pound regular or maple-flavored bulk pork sausage
2 acorn squash (about 2 pounds each)
1 cup cooked rice
½ cup dried cranberries
½ teaspoon salt
½ teaspoon ground cinnamon
½ teaspoon black pepper
1 can (10¾ ounces) condensed chicken broth, divided

1. Preheat oven to 350°F. Grease 11×7-inch baking dish.

2. Heat large skillet over medium-high heat. Crumble sausage into skillet; cook and stir 5 minutes or until browned. Drain fat. Place sausage in large bowl.

3. Meanwhile, pierce both squash in several places using sharp knife. Microwave on HIGH 8 minutes, turning over halfway through cooking time. When cool enough to handle, cut ½ inch off top and bottom of each squash. Cut each squash horizontally. Remove seeds and membrane. Place squash rings in prepared baking dish.

4. Add rice, cranberries, salt, cinnamon and pepper to sausage. Stir in ¼ cup broth. Spoon sausage mixture into squash rings. Pour remaining broth into baking dish around squash.

5. Bake, covered, 15 minutes. Bake, uncovered, 5 to 10 minutes or until squash is tender.

Makes 4 servings

Pork Chop & Wild Rice Bake

1 package (6 ounces) seasoned long grain & wild rice mix
1⅓ cups FRENCH'S® French Fried Onions, divided
1 package (10 ounces) frozen cut green beans, thawed and drained
¼ cup orange juice
1 teaspoon grated orange peel
4 boneless pork chops (1 inch thick)

1. Preheat oven to 375°F. Combine rice mix and seasoning packet, *2 cups water,* *⅔ cup* French Fried Onions, green beans, orange juice and orange peel in 2-quart shallow baking dish. Arrange pork chops on top.

2. Bake, uncovered, 30 minutes or until pork chops are no longer pink in center. Sprinkle chops with remaining *⅔ cup* onions. Bake 5 minutes or until onions are golden.

Makes 4 servings

Harvest Casserole

Manicotti Cordon Bleu

  1 package (12 ounces) SARGENTO® String Cheese Snacks
12 slices deli ham or turkey
12 manicotti pasta shells, uncooked
  1 jar (26 ounces) pasta sauce
  ¾ cup water
  ½ cup (2 ounces) SARGENTO® ARTISAN BLENDS™ Shredded Parmesan Cheese

1. Unwrap cheese snacks; place over each meat slice and roll up. Slide rolled cheese snack into pasta shell.

2. Combine pasta sauce and water; mix well. Spread ¾ cup sauce mixture over bottom of 13×9-inch baking dish. Arrange filled pasta shells in dish; spread remaining sauce mixture evenly over shells. Cover with foil; bake in preheated 350°F oven 50 minutes or until pasta is tender. Top with Parmesan cheese.

Makes 4 servings

Prep Time: 15 minutes
Bake Time: 50 minutes

Autumn Veg•All® Pot Pie

  1 jar (12 ounces) pork gravy
  ¼ cup honey mustard
  1 can (15 ounces) VEG•ALL® Original Mixed Vegetables, drained
  2 cups cooked pork (tenderloin, loin or roast), cubed
  ¼ teaspoon dried thyme leaves
  1 medium tart apple, peeled, seeded and chopped
  1 small onion, chopped
  1 sheet puff pastry dough
  1 large egg, beaten

Preheat oven to 375°F.

In a large bowl, whisk together gravy and honey mustard. Add Veg•All, pork, thyme, apple and onion. Toss to coat. Transfer mixture to greased 10-inch pie plate.

Roll out puff pastry dough to fit pie plate. Brush egg around rim of plate. Place puff pastry over pork mixture and press edges to seal. Trim edges. Cut 3 to 4 slits in top for venting. Bake 50 to 60 minutes or until golden brown.   Makes 6 to 8 servings

Note: This recipe works well with leftover grilled meat.

Manicotti Cordon Bleu

Hungarian Goulash Casserole

1 pound ground pork
¼ teaspoon salt
¼ teaspoon ground nutmeg
¼ teaspoon black pepper
1 tablespoon vegetable oil
1 cup sour cream, divided
1 tablespoon cornstarch
1 can (10¾ ounces) cream of celery soup, undiluted
1 cup milk
1 teaspoon sweet Hungarian paprika
1 package (12 ounces) egg noodles, cooked and drained
2 teaspoons minced fresh dill (optional)

1. Preheat oven to 325°F. Spray 3-quart casserole with nonstick cooking spray.

2. Combine pork, salt, nutmeg and pepper in medium bowl; shape into 1-inch balls. Heat oil in large skillet over medium-high heat. Add meatballs; cook 10 minutes or until browned on all sides and no longer pink in center. Remove meatballs from skillet; discard drippings.

3. Stir ¼ cup sour cream and cornstarch in small bowl. Spoon into same skillet. Add remaining ¾ cup sour cream, soup, milk and paprika; cook and stir over medium heat until smooth. *Do not boil.* Spread noodles in prepared casserole. Arrange meatballs over noodles and top with sauce.

4. Bake 20 minutes or until heated through. Garnish with dill.

Makes 4 to 6 servings

Hungarian Goulash Casserole

Sunday Supper Stuffed Shells

1 package (12 ounces) uncooked jumbo pasta shells

2 tablespoons olive oil

3 cloves garlic, halved

¾ pound ground veal

¾ pound ground pork

1 package (10 ounces) frozen chopped spinach, thawed and squeezed dry

1 cup fresh parsley, finely chopped

1 cup dry bread crumbs

2 eggs, beaten

3 tablespoons grated Parmesan cheese

3 cloves garlic, minced

   Salt

3 cups pasta sauce

1. Preheat oven to 375°F. Grease 12×8-inch baking pan.

2. Cook shells according to package directions; drain.

3. Heat oil in large skillet over medium heat. Add halved garlic cloves; cook and stir until lightly browned. Discard garlic. Brown veal and pork in skillet, stirring to break up meat. Drain fat. Cool slightly.

4. Combine spinach, parsley, bread crumbs, eggs, cheese and minced garlic in large bowl; blend well. Season with salt. Add meat; blend well. Fill shells with meat mixture. Spread about 1 cup pasta sauce over bottom of prepared pan. Arrange shells in pan. Pour remaining pasta sauce over shells.

5. Bake, covered, 35 to 45 minutes or until hot and bubbly.   Makes 8 servings

Oven Pork Cassoulet

1 tablespoon canola oil

1¼ pounds pork tenderloin, trimmed of fat and cut into 1-inch pieces

1 cup chopped onion

1 cup chopped carrots

3 cloves garlic, minced

2 cans (about 15 ounces each) cannellini beans, rinsed and drained

1 can (about 14 ounces) diced tomatoes with Italian seasoning

¼ pound smoked turkey sausage, cut into ¼-inch-thick slices

1 teaspoon dried thyme

¼ teaspoon salt

¼ teaspoon dried rosemary

¼ teaspoon black pepper

1. Preheat oven to 325°F.

2. Heat oil in Dutch oven over medium heat; brown pork in batches. Transfer pork to plate.

3. Add onion, carrots and garlic to Dutch oven; cook and stir 8 to 10 minutes or until tender. Combine pork, onion mixture, beans, tomatoes, sausage, thyme, salt, rosemary and pepper in 3-quart casserole.

4. Bake, covered, 35 to 40 minutes or until pork is barely pink in center.

Makes 6 servings

tip

A Dutch oven is a large, heavy covered pot with two short handles that is used for the slow, moist cooking of a large quantity of food. It is ideal for braising large pieces of meat. Choose one with ovenproof handles if you would like the convenience of using it in the oven as well as on the stovetop. Dutch ovens range in size from 5 to 8 quarts.

Oven Pork Cassoulet

Savory Vegetable Stuffing Bake

¼ pound bulk pork sausage

1 large onion, chopped (about 1 cup)

½ teaspoon dried thyme leaves, crushed

1 can (10¾ ounces) CAMPBELL'S® Condensed Cream of Celery Soup (Regular or 98% Fat Free)

1 can (about 8 ounces) stewed tomatoes

2 cups frozen vegetable combination (broccoli, corn, red pepper)

3 cups PEPPERIDGE FARM® Herb Seasoned Stuffing

1. Cook the sausage, onion and thyme in a 12-inch skillet over medium-high heat until the sausage is browned, stirring frequently to break up the meat. Pour off any fat.

2. Stir the soup, tomatoes and vegetables in the skillet. Heat to a boil. Remove the skillet from the heat. Add the stuffing and stir lightly to coat. Spoon into a 1½-quart casserole.

3. Bake at 350°F. for 30 minutes or until it is hot and bubbling.   Makes 6 servings

Prep Time: 20 minutes
Bake Time: 30 minutes
Total Time: 50 minutes

Classic Tuna Noodle Casserole

**1 can (10¾ ounces) CAMPBELL'S® Condensed Cream of Celery Soup
    (Regular or 98% Fat Free)**
½ cup milk
1 cup cooked peas
2 tablespoons chopped pimientos
2 cans (about 6 ounces each) tuna, drained and flaked
2 cups hot cooked medium egg noodles
2 tablespoons dry bread crumbs
1 tablespoon butter, melted

1. Heat the oven to 400°F. Stir the soup, milk, peas, pimientos, tuna and noodles in a 1½-quart baking dish. Stir the bread crumbs and butter in a small bowl.

2. Bake for 20 minutes or until the tuna mixture is hot and bubbling. Stir the tuna mixture. Sprinkle with the bread crumb mixture.

3. Bake for 5 minutes or until the bread crumbs are golden brown.

Makes 4 servings

Prep Time: 10 minutes
Bake Time: 25 minutes
Total Time: 35 minutes

Serving Suggestion: Serve with your favorite vegetable combination. For dessert serve ice cream.
Kitchen Tip: Substitute Campbell's® Condensed Cream of Mushroom Soup for the Cream of Celery Soup.

Crab and Corn Enchilada Casserole

Spicy Tomato Sauce (recipe follows), divided
10 to 12 ounces crabmeat, fresh, frozen or pasteurized
1 package (10 ounces) frozen corn, thawed and drained
1½ cups (6 ounces) shredded Monterey Jack cheese, divided
1 can (4 ounces) diced mild green chiles
12 (6-inch) corn tortillas
1 lime, cut into 6 wedges
Sour cream (optional)

1. Prepare Spicy Tomato Sauce. Preheat oven to 350°F.

2. Pick out and discard any shell or cartilage from crabmeat. Combine 2 cups Spicy Tomato Sauce, crabmeat, corn, 1 cup cheese and chiles in medium bowl. Cut each tortilla into 4 wedges. Place one third of tortilla wedges in shallow 3- to 4-quart casserole, overlapping to make solid layer. Spread half of crab mixture on top. Repeat with another layer of tortilla wedges, remaining crab mixture and remaining tortillas. Spread remaining 1 cup Spicy Tomato Sauce over top.

3. Bake, covered, 30 to 40 minutes or until heated through. Sprinkle with remaining ½ cup cheese. Bake 5 minutes or until cheese melts. Squeeze lime over individual servings. Serve with sour cream, if desired. Makes 6 servings

Spicy Tomato Sauce

6 medium tomatoes
2 teaspoons olive oil
1 medium onion, chopped
1 tablespoon minced garlic
2 tablespoons chili powder
2 teaspoons *each* ground cumin and dried oregano
1 teaspoon ground cinnamon
¼ teaspoon *each* red pepper flakes and ground cloves

1. Place tomatoes in food processor or blender; process until finely chopped.

2. Heat oil in large saucepan or Dutch oven over medium-high heat. Add onion and garlic; cook and stir 5 minutes or until onion is tender. Stir in tomatoes, chili powder, cumin, oregano, cinnamon, red pepper flakes and cloves. Reduce heat to medium-low. Simmer 20 minutes or until sauce is reduced to 3 cups. Makes 3 cups

Crab and Corn Enchilada Casserole

Salmon and Dill Penne Casserole

4 ounces uncooked multigrain penne pasta
2 tablespoons all-purpose flour
¾ cup chicken broth
½ cup milk
1 teaspoon dried dill weed
1 cup frozen baby peas, thawed
1 can (7½ ounces) red salmon
½ cup panko bread crumbs
¼ cup grated Parmesan cheese

1. Preheat oven to 375°F.

2. Cook pasta according to package directions; drain.

3. Place flour in medium saucepan over medium heat. Gradually whisk in broth and milk until smooth; bring to a boil. Reduce heat to low. Simmer 2 minutes or until thickened, whisking constantly. Stir in dill weed; remove from heat. Stir in pasta and peas; mix well.

4. Drain salmon; break into large chunks and discard skin and bones. Gently fold salmon into pasta mixture. Transfer mixture to shallow 1½-quart baking dish. Top with panko and cheese.

5. Bake 12 to 15 minutes or until bubbly.   Makes 4 servings

tip

Panko bread crumbs are light, crispy, Japanese-style bread crumbs. They can be found in the Asian aisle of most supermarkets. Unseasoned dry bread crumbs can be substituted.

Shrimp Noodle Supreme

1 package (8 ounces) spinach noodles, cooked and drained

3 ounces cream cheese, cubed and softened

½ cup (1 stick) butter

1½ pounds medium raw shrimp, peeled

Salt and black pepper

1 can (10¾ ounces) condensed cream of mushroom soup, undiluted

1 cup sour cream

½ cup half-and-half

½ cup mayonnaise

1 tablespoon snipped chives, plus additional for garnish

1 tablespoon chopped fresh parsley, plus additional for garnish

½ teaspoon Dijon mustard

¾ cup (3 ounces) shredded sharp Cheddar cheese

1. Preheat oven to 325°F. Spray 13×9-inch casserole with nonstick cooking spray.

2. Combine noodles and cream cheese in medium bowl. Spread noodle mixture in bottom of prepared casserole. Melt butter in large skillet over medium-high heat. Add shrimp; cook 5 minutes or until pink and opaque. Season with salt and pepper. Layer shrimp over noodles.

3. Combine soup, sour cream, half-and-half, mayonnaise, 1 tablespoon chives, 1 tablespoon parsley and mustard in another medium bowl. Spread over shrimp. Sprinkle Cheddar cheese over top.

4. Bake 25 minutes or until cheese is melted. Garnish with additional chives and parsley.   Makes 6 servings

Shrimp Noodle Supreme

Fish Broccoli Casserole

1 package (10 ounces) frozen broccoli spears, thawed, drained
1 cup cooked flaked Florida whitefish
1 can (10¾ ounces) condensed cream of mushroom soup, undiluted
½ cup milk
¼ teaspoon salt
⅛ teaspoon freshly ground black pepper
½ cup crushed potato chips

Preheat oven to 425°F. Grease 1½-quart casserole. Layer broccoli in prepared casserole. Combine fish, soup, milk, salt and pepper in large bowl.

Spread fish mixture over broccoli. Sprinkle with potato chips. Bake 12 to 15 minutes or until golden brown.   Makes 4 servings

Favorite recipe from **Florida Department of Agriculture and Consumer Services, Bureau of Seafood and Aquaculture**

Citrus Baked Flounder

1⅓ cups FRENCH'S® French Fried Onions, divided
1 teaspoon grated lemon peel
2 cups cooked white rice
2 tablespoons butter or margarine, melted
2 tablespoons lemon juice
4 flounder fillets, about 1 pound
   Salt and black pepper to taste
   Chopped parsley (optional)

1. Preheat oven to 350°F. Stir ⅔ *cup* French Fried Onions and lemon peel into cooked rice. Mix butter and lemon juice; set aside.

2. Spoon rice mixture into lightly greased 9-inch square baking dish. Arrange fish on top of rice, folding fillets to fit if necessary. Season with salt and pepper to taste. Drizzle with butter mixture.

3. Bake 20 minutes. Sprinkle with remaining ⅔ *cup* onions. Bake 5 minutes or until fish is opaque and onions are golden. Garnish with parsley, if desired.

Makes 4 servings

Prep Time: 10 minutes
Bake Time: 25 minutes

Baked Red Snappers with Veg•All®

2 pounds red snapper
1 small onion, minced
½ green pepper, minced
1 jalapeño (with seeds), minced
½ cup black olives, sliced
4 garlic cloves, minced
1 can (15 ounces) VEG•ALL® Original Mixed Vegetables, drained
2 cups cooked rice
½ teaspoon salt
¼ teaspoon pepper

Preheat oven to 400°F.

Lightly grease oven-proof casserole dish.

Place snapper in casserole dish without crowding.

In medium bowl, mix onion, green pepper, jalapeño, black olives and garlic.

Stir in Veg•All, rice, salt and pepper.

Lightly stuff cavities of snapper with filling. Place remaining filling around snapper.

Bake 20 minutes.   Makes 4 servings

tip

Jalapeño peppers can sting and irritate the skin, so wear rubber gloves when handling peppers and do not touch your eyes.

Company Crab

1 pound Florida blue crabmeat, fresh, frozen or pasteurized
1 can (15 ounces) artichoke hearts, drained
1 can (4 ounces) sliced mushrooms, drained
2 tablespoons butter or margarine
2½ tablespoons all-purpose flour
½ teaspoon salt
⅛ teaspoon ground red pepper
1 cup half-and-half
2 tablespoons dry sherry
2 tablespoons crushed cornflakes
1 tablespoon grated Parmesan cheese
Paprika

Preheat oven to 450°F. Thaw crabmeat if frozen. Remove any pieces of shell or cartilage. Cut artichoke hearts in half; place artichokes in well-greased, shallow 1½-quart casserole. Add crabmeat and mushrooms; cover and set aside.

Melt butter in small saucepan over medium heat. Stir in flour, salt and ground red pepper. Gradually stir in half-and-half. Continue cooking until sauce thickens, stirring constantly. Stir in sherry. Pour sauce over crabmeat. Combine cornflakes and cheese in small bowl; sprinkle over casserole. Sprinkle with paprika. Bake 12 to 15 minutes or until bubbly. Makes 6 servings

Favorite recipe from **Florida Department of Agriculture and Consumer Services, Bureau of Seafood and Aquaculture**

Scallop and Artichoke Heart Casserole

1 package (9 ounces) frozen artichoke hearts, cooked and drained
1 pound scallops
1 teaspoon vegetable oil
¼ cup chopped red bell pepper
¼ cup sliced green onions
¼ cup all-purpose flour
2 cups milk
1 teaspoon dried tarragon
¼ teaspoon salt
¼ teaspoon white pepper
1 tablespoon chopped fresh parsley
Dash paprika

1. Preheat oven to 350°F.

2. Cut large artichoke hearts lengthwise into halves. Arrange artichoke hearts in even layer in 8-inch square baking dish.

3. Rinse scallops; pat dry with paper towel. If scallops are large, cut into halves. Arrange scallops evenly over artichokes.

4. Heat oil in medium saucepan over medium-low heat. Add bell pepper and green onions; cook and stir 5 minutes or until tender. Stir in flour. Gradually stir in milk until smooth. Add tarragon, salt and white pepper; cook and stir over medium heat 10 minutes or until sauce boils and thickens. Pour sauce over scallops.

5. Bake 25 minutes or until bubbly and scallops are opaque. Sprinkle with parsley and paprika.

Makes 4 servings

Scallop and Artichoke Heart Casserole

Seafood Pasta

½ cup olive oil
1 pound asparagus, trimmed and cut into 1-inch pieces
1 cup chopped green onions
1 tablespoon plus 2 teaspoons minced garlic
1 package (16 ounces) linguine, cooked and drained
1 pound medium cooked shrimp, peeled
1 package (8 ounces) imitation crabmeat
1 package (8 ounces) imitation lobster
1 can (8 ounces) pitted black olives, drained

1. Preheat oven to 350°F. Spray 4-quart casserole with nonstick cooking spray.

2. Heat oil in large skillet over medium heat. Add asparagus, green onions and garlic; cook and stir until tender. Combine asparagus mixture, linguine, shrimp, crabmeat, lobster and olives in prepared casserole.

3. Bake 30 minutes or until heated through.   Makes 6 servings

Sole Almondine

1 package (6.5 ounces) RICE-A-RONI® Broccoli Au Gratin
1 medium zucchini
4 sole, scrod or orange roughy fillets
1 tablespoon lemon juice
¼ cup grated Parmesan cheese, divided
   Salt and pepper (optional)
¼ cup sliced almonds
2 tablespoons margarine or butter, melted

1. Prepare Rice-A-Roni® Mix as package directs.

2. Meanwhile, cut zucchini lengthwise into 12 thin strips. Heat oven to 350°F.

3. In 11×7-inch glass baking dish, spread prepared rice evenly. Set aside. Sprinkle fish with lemon juice, 2 tablespoons cheese, salt and pepper, if desired. Place zucchini strips over fish; roll up. Place fish seam-side down on rice.

4. Combine almonds and margarine; sprinkle evenly over fish. Top with remaining 2 tablespoons cheese. Bake 20 to 25 minutes or until fish flakes easily with fork.
                    Makes 4 servings

Jambalaya

1 teaspoon vegetable oil
½ pound smoked deli ham, cubed
½ pound smoked sausage, cut into ¼-inch-thick slices
1 large onion, chopped
1 large green bell pepper, chopped
3 stalks celery, chopped
3 cloves garlic, minced
1 can (about 28 ounces) diced tomatoes
1 can (about 14 ounces) chicken broth
1 cup uncooked rice
1 tablespoon Worcestershire sauce
1 teaspoon salt
1 teaspoon dried thyme
½ teaspoon black pepper
¼ teaspoon ground red pepper
1 package (12 ounces) frozen medium raw shrimp, peeled, thawed
   Fresh chives (optional)

1. Preheat oven to 350°F. Spray 13×9-inch baking dish with nonstick cooking spray.

2. Heat oil in large skillet over medium-high heat. Add ham and sausage; cook and stir 5 minutes or until sausage is lightly browned. Transfer to prepared dish. Place onion, bell pepper, celery and garlic in same skillet; cook and stir 3 minutes. Add to sausage mixture.

3. Combine tomatoes, broth, rice, Worcestershire sauce, salt, thyme, black pepper and red pepper in same skillet; bring to a boil over high heat. Reduce heat to low and simmer 3 minutes. Pour tomato mixture over sausage mixture; stir until combined.

4. Bake, covered, 45 minutes or until rice is almost tender. Place shrimp on top of rice mixture. Bake, uncovered, 10 minutes or until shrimp are pink and opaque. Garnish with chives.

Makes 8 servings

Jambalaya

Mediterranean-Style Tuna Noodle Casserole

1 tablespoon extra-virgin olive oil
4 cloves garlic, minced
2 large onions, chopped (1½ cups)
12 ounces mushrooms, chopped (4 cups)
2 large tomatoes, chopped
1 red bell pepper, diced (1 cup)
1 green bell pepper, diced (1 cup)
1 cup chopped fresh cilantro leaves *or* ¼ cup dried oregano leaves
2 tablespoons dried marjoram or oregano leaves
1 to 2 teaspoons ground red pepper
1 pound JARLSBERG LITE™ cheese, shredded (4 cups)
1 (16-ounce) can black-eyed peas, rinsed and drained
2 (7-ounce) cans tuna, drained and flaked
6 ounces cooked pasta (tricolor rotelle, bows or macaroni)

Preheat oven to 350°F. Heat oil in large skillet; sauté garlic until golden. Add onions; sauté until transparent, about 2 minutes on medium-high heat.

Add mushrooms, tomatoes and bell peppers; cook and stir 3 to 5 minutes or until mushrooms begin to brown. Add cilantro, marjoram and ground red pepper.

Toss with cheese, peas, tuna and pasta. Pour into greased baking dish. Bake, covered, 45 minutes or until cooked through.   Makes 6 to 8 servings

Mediterranean-Style Tuna Noodle Casserole

Broccoli Fish Roll-Ups

1 can (10¾ ounces) cream of broccoli soup, undiluted
½ cup milk
2 cups seasoned stuffing mix
4 flounder fillets (about 3 ounces each)
1 package (10 ounces) frozen broccoli spears, thawed
   Paprika

1. Preheat oven to 375°F. Spray 9-inch square baking dish with nonstick cooking spray.

2. Combine soup and milk in medium bowl. Reserve ½ cup soup mixture; set aside.

3. Combine stuffing mix and remaining soup mixture in medium bowl; pat into prepared dish.

4. Place fish on clean work surface. Arrange 1 broccoli spear crosswise across narrow end of 1 fillet. Starting at narrow end, gently roll up fish. Place over stuffing mixture, seam side down. Repeat with remaining fish and broccoli.

5. Arrange any remaining broccoli spears over stuffing mixture. Spoon reserved ½ cup soup mixture over roll-ups. Sprinkle with paprika.

6. Bake 20 minutes or until fish begins to flake when tested with fork.

Makes 4 servings

tip Asparagus spears and cream of asparagus soup can be substituted for the broccoli spears and broccoli soup.

Broccoli Fish Roll-Up

Lemon Shrimp

1 package (12 ounces) uncooked egg noodles
½ cup (1 stick) butter, softened
2 pounds medium cooked shrimp, peeled
3 tomatoes, chopped
1 cup shredded carrots
1 cup chicken broth
1 can (4 ounces) sliced mushrooms, drained
2 tablespoons lemon juice
2 cloves garlic, minced
½ teaspoon celery seed
¼ teaspoon black pepper

1. Preheat oven to 350°F.

2. Cook noodles according to package directions; drain. Toss with butter in large bowl until butter is melted and noodles are evenly coated. Stir in shrimp, tomatoes, carrots, broth, mushrooms, lemon juice, garlic, celery seed and pepper. Transfer to 3-quart casserole.

3. Bake 15 to 20 minutes or until heated through.   Makes 8 servings

Salmon Veg•All® Pasta Bake

3 cups cooked small shell pasta
1 can (14¾ ounces) pink salmon, drained or 1 pound cooked salmon
1 can (15 ounces) VEG•ALL® Original Mixed Vegetables, drained
1 can (10¾ ounces) condensed cream of mushroom soup
¼ teaspoon pepper
½ cup dry bread crumbs

Preheat oven to 350°F.

In large bowl, combine pasta, salmon, Veg•All, soup and pepper.

Pour into greased 3-quart casserole.

Bake 25 minutes or until hot. Sprinkle bread crumbs over top; bake, uncovered, 10 minutes more.   Makes 6 servings

Lemon Shrimp

Louisiana Seafood Bake

1 can (14½ ounces) whole tomatoes, undrained and cut up

1 can (8 ounces) tomato sauce

1 cup water

1 cup sliced celery

⅔ cup uncooked regular rice

1⅓ cups FRENCH'S® French Fried Onions, divided

1 teaspoon FRANK'S® REDHOT® Original Cayenne Pepper Sauce

½ teaspoon garlic powder

¼ teaspoon dried oregano, crumbled

¼ teaspoon dried thyme, crumbled

½ pound white fish, thawed if frozen and cut into 1-inch chunks

1 can (4 ounces) shrimp, drained

⅓ cup sliced pitted ripe olives

¼ cup (1 ounce) grated Parmesan cheese

1. Preheat oven to 375°F.

2. In 1½-quart casserole, combine tomatoes, tomato sauce, water, celery, uncooked rice, ⅔ cup French Fried Onions and seasonings.

3. Bake, covered, 20 minutes. Stir in fish, shrimp and olives. Bake, covered, 20 minutes or until heated through. Top with cheese and remaining ⅔ cup onions; bake, uncovered, 3 minutes or until onions are golden brown.   Makes 4 servings

Microwave Directions: In 2-quart microwave-safe casserole, prepare rice mixture as above. Cook, covered, on HIGH 15 minutes, stirring rice halfway through cooking time. Add fish, shrimp and olives. Cook, covered, 12 to 14 minutes or until rice is cooked. Stir casserole halfway through cooking time. Top with cheese and remaining ⅔ cup onions; cook, uncovered, 1 minute. Let stand 5 minutes.

Louisiana Seafood Bake

Curried Fish Casserole

2 cups thinly sliced bok choy or napa cabbage
1 cup sliced red bell pepper, divided
½ cup uncooked quick-cooking brown rice
⅓ cup plus 3 tablespoons water, divided
4 tilapia or whitefish fillets (¼ pound each)
Salt
1 cup chicken broth
1 teaspoon curry powder
¾ teaspoon sugar
1 tablespoon cornstarch
¼ cup finely chopped green onions (optional)

1. Preheat oven to 350°F. Spray 13×9-inch baking dish with nonstick cooking spray.

2. Combine bok choy, ½ cup bell pepper, rice and ⅓ cup water in prepared dish; toss gently to blend. Arrange fish over vegetables; sprinkle with salt.

3. Bake, covered, 30 minutes or until fish begins to flake when tested with fork.

4. Meanwhile, combine broth, remaining ½ cup bell pepper, curry powder, sugar and salt in small saucepan; bring to a boil over medium-high heat. Cook and stir 1 minute.

5. Combine cornstarch and remaining 3 tablespoons water in small bowl; stir until completely dissolved. Add to broth mixture; cook and stir 1 minute or until thickened.

6. Serve fish over rice and vegetable mixture. Spoon sauce over top. Garnish with green onions.

Makes 4 servings

Curried Fish Casserole

Impossibly Easy Salmon Pie

1 can (7½ ounces) red salmon, drained and deboned
½ cup grated Parmesan cheese
¼ cup sliced green onions
1 jar (2 ounces) chopped pimientos, drained
½ cup cottage cheese
1 tablespoon lemon juice
1½ cups milk
¾ cup biscuit baking mix
2 eggs
2 egg whites
¼ teaspoon salt
¼ teaspoon dried dill weed
¼ teaspoon paprika (optional)

1. Preheat oven to 375°F. Spray 9-inch pie plate with nonstick cooking spray.

2. Combine salmon, Parmesan cheese, green onions and pimientos in prepared pie plate.

3. Combine cottage cheese and lemon juice in blender or food processor; blend until smooth. Add milk, baking mix, eggs, egg whites, salt and dill weed; blend 15 seconds. Pour over salmon mixture in pie plate. Sprinkle with paprika, if desired.

4. Bake 35 to 40 minutes or until lightly golden and knife inserted near center comes out clean. Let stand 5 minutes before serving.   Makes 8 servings

Impossibly Easy Salmon Pie

Gumbo Casserole

2 cans (10¾ ounces each) CAMPBELL'S® Condensed Light Soups
   Chicken Gumbo Soup
1 soup can water
1 teaspoon dried minced onion
½ teaspoon Cajun seasoning
½ teaspoon garlic powder
1 cup frozen okra, thawed
¾ cup uncooked instant white rice
½ pound cooked ham, diced (about 1½ cups)
½ pound cooked shrimp, peeled and deveined

1. Heat the oven to 375°F. Stir the soup, water, onion, Cajun seasoning, garlic powder, okra, rice, ham and shrimp in a 2-quart casserole.

2. Bake for 35 minutes or until the gumbo is hot and bubbling. Stir the gumbo before serving.

Makes 4 servings

Prep Time: 15 minutes
Bake Time: 35 minutes
Total Time: 50 minutes

Cheesy Tuna Pie

2 cups cooked rice
2 cans (6 ounces each) tuna, drained and flaked
1 cup mayonnaise
1 cup (4 ounces) shredded Cheddar cheese
½ cup thinly sliced celery
½ cup sour cream
1 can (4 ounces) sliced black olives
2 tablespoons dried minced onion
1 refrigerated pie crust (half of 15-ounce package)

1. Preheat oven to 350°F. Spray 9-inch deep-dish pie pan with nonstick cooking spray.

2. Combine rice, tuna, mayonnaise, cheese, celery, sour cream, olives and onion in medium bowl; mix well. Spoon into prepared pan. Top with pie crust; press edge to pan to seal. Cut slits for steam to escape.

3. Bake 20 minutes or until crust is browned and filling is bubbly.

Makes 6 servings

Gumbo Casserole

Seafood Newburg Casserole

1 can (10¾ ounces) condensed cream of shrimp soup, undiluted
½ cup half-and-half
1 tablespoon dry sherry
¼ teaspoon ground red pepper
2 cans (6 ounces each) lump crabmeat, drained
3 cups cooked rice
¼ pound medium raw shrimp, peeled
¼ pound bay scallops, rinsed and patted dry
1 jar (4 ounces) pimientos, drained and chopped
¼ cup finely chopped fresh parsley

1. Preheat oven to 350°F. Spray 2½-quart casserole with nonstick cooking spray.

2. Whisk soup, half-and-half, sherry and red pepper in large bowl until blended. Pick out and discard any shell or cartilage from crabmeat. Add crabmeat, rice, shrimp, scallops and pimientos to soup mixture; mix well. Transfer mixture to prepared casserole.

3. Bake, covered, 25 minutes or until shrimp and scallops are opaque. Sprinkle with parsley.   Makes 6 servings

Seafood Newburg Casserole

Crustless Salmon & Broccoli Quiche

3 eggs

¼ cup chopped green onions

¼ cup plain yogurt

2 teaspoons all-purpose flour

1 teaspoon dried basil

Salt and black pepper

¾ cup frozen broccoli florets, thawed and drained

1 can (6 ounces) boneless skinless salmon, drained and flaked

2 tablespoons grated Parmesan cheese

1 plum tomato, thinly sliced

¼ cup fresh bread crumbs

1. Preheat oven to 375°F. Spray 1½-quart casserole or 9-inch deep-dish pie plate with nonstick cooking spray.

2. Combine eggs, green onions, yogurt, flour, basil, salt and pepper in medium bowl until well blended. Stir in broccoli, salmon and cheese. Spread evenly in prepared casserole. Top with tomato slices and sprinkle with bread crumbs.

3. Bake 20 to 25 minutes or until knife inserted near center comes out clean. Let stand 5 minutes before serving.   Makes 4 servings

tip

Quiches can easily be prepared with a variety of fillings. Try using spinach or asparagus instead of the broccoli. In place of the Parmesan cheese, you may want to try Swiss, Cheddar, Monterey Jack or Colby.

Crustless Salmon & Broccoli Quiche

Shrimp and Chicken Paella

¾ cup cooked rice
2 cans (about 14 ounces each) diced tomatoes
½ teaspoon ground turmeric *or* **⅛ teaspoon saffron threads**
1 package (12 ounces) medium raw shrimp, peeled
2 chicken tenders (about 4 ounces), cut into 1-inch pieces
1 cup frozen peas

1. Preheat oven to 400°F. Lightly coat 8-inch square baking dish with nonstick cooking spray.

2. Spread rice in prepared dish. Pour 1 can of tomatoes with juice over rice; sprinkle turmeric over tomatoes. Arrange shrimp and chicken over tomatoes. Top with peas. Drain remaining can of tomatoes, discarding juice. Spread tomatoes evenly over shrimp and chicken.

3. Bake, covered, 30 minutes. Let stand 5 minutes before serving.

Makes 4 servings

Flounder Fillets over Zesty Lemon Rice

¼ cup (½ stick) butter
3 tablespoons lemon juice
2 teaspoons chicken bouillon granules
½ teaspoon black pepper
1 cup cooked rice
1 package (10 ounces) frozen chopped broccoli, thawed
1 cup (4 ounces) shredded sharp Cheddar cheese
1 pound flounder fillets
½ teaspoon paprika

1. Preheat oven to 375°F. Spray 2-quart casserole with nonstick cooking spray.

2. Melt butter in small saucepan over medium heat. Add lemon juice, bouillon granules and pepper; cook and stir 2 minutes or until bouillon granules dissolve.

3. Combine rice, broccoli, cheese and ¼ cup lemon sauce in medium bowl; spread on bottom of prepared dish. Place fish over rice mixture. Pour remaining lemon sauce over fish.

4. Bake 20 minutes or until fish begins to flake when tested with fork. Sprinkle with paprika.

Makes 6 servings

Shrimp and Chicken Paella

Seafood Lasagna

1 package (16 ounces) uncooked lasagna noodles

2 tablespoons butter

1 large onion, finely chopped

1½ cups cottage cheese

1 package (8 ounces) cream cheese, cut into ½-inch pieces, softened

1 egg, lightly beaten

2 teaspoons dried basil

Salt and black pepper

2 cans (10¾ ounces each) cream of mushroom soup, undiluted

⅓ cup milk

1 clove garlic, minced

½ pound bay scallops, rinsed and patted dry

½ pound flounder fillets, rinsed, patted dry and cut into ½-inch cubes

½ pound medium raw shrimp, peeled

½ cup dry white wine

1 cup (4 ounces) shredded mozzarella cheese

2 tablespoons grated Parmesan cheese

1. Cook lasagna noodles according to package directions; drain.

2. Melt butter in large skillet over medium heat. Add onion; cook and stir until tender. Remove from heat. Stir in cottage cheese, cream cheese, egg, basil, salt and pepper; mix well.

3. Combine soups, milk and garlic in large bowl until well blended. Stir in scallops, flounder, shrimp and wine.

4. Preheat oven to 350°F. Grease 13×9-inch baking pan.

5. Place layer of lasagna noodles in prepared pan, overlapping edges. Spread half of cheese mixture over noodles. Place layer of noodles over cheese mixture and top with half of seafood mixture. Repeat layers. Sprinkle with mozzarella and Parmesan cheeses.

6. Bake 45 minutes or until hot and bubbly. Let stand 15 minutes before serving.

Makes 8 to 10 servings

Seafood Lasagna

Easy Crab-Asparagus Pie

      4 ounces crabmeat, fresh, frozen or pasteurized
  1½ cups sliced asparagus, cooked
    ½ cup chopped onion, cooked
    1 cup (4 ounces) shredded Monterey Jack cheese
    ¼ cup grated Parmesan cheese
      Black pepper
    ¾ cup all-purpose flour
    ¾ teaspoon baking powder
    ½ teaspoon salt
    2 tablespoons butter
  1½ cups milk
    4 eggs, lightly beaten

1. Preheat oven to 350°F. Lightly grease 10-inch quiche dish or pie plate.

2. Pick out and discard any shell or cartilage from crabmeat. Layer crabmeat, asparagus and onion in prepared dish; top with cheeses. Season with pepper.

3. Combine flour, baking powder and salt in large bowl. Cut in butter with pastry blender or two knives until mixture forms coarse crumbs. Stir in milk and eggs; pour over crabmeat mixture and cheeses.

4. Bake 30 minutes or until puffed and knife inserted near center comes out clean.

Makes 6 servings

Seafood Enchiladas

½ **pound cleaned shrimp, chopped**
1 **can (6 ounces) crabmeat, drained, flaked**
1 **can (7 ounces) whole kernel corn, drained**
½ **cup chopped green onions (about 2)**
½ **teaspoon ground red pepper (cayenne), divided**
1 **package (8 ounces) KRAFT® 2% Milk Shredded Cheddar Cheese, divided**
10 **flour tortillas (7 inch)**
4 **ounces (½ of 8-ounce package) PHILADELPHIA® Cream Cheese, cubed**
¾ **cup milk**

HEAT oven to 350°F.

COOK and stir shrimp in medium nonstick skillet sprayed with cooking spray on medium heat 2 minutes. Add crabmeat, corn, onions and ¼ teaspoon of the pepper; mix well. Cook and stir an additional 2 minutes or until shrimp turn pink. Remove from heat. Stir in 1 cup of the shredded cheese.

SPOON ⅓ cup of the seafood mixture onto each tortilla; roll up. Place, seam-sides down, in lightly greased 13×9-inch baking dish. Place cream cheese in medium saucepan. Add milk; cook on medium-low heat 5 minutes or until cream cheese is completely melted and mixture is well blended, stirring frequently. Pour evenly over enchiladas.

BAKE 5 minutes. Remove from oven. Sprinkle with remaining shredded cheese. Bake an additional 5 minutes or until cheese is melted. Sprinkle with remaining ¼ teaspoon pepper. Makes 10 servings

Prep Time: 20 minutes
Bake Time: 10 minutes
Total Time: 30 minutes

Salmon & Noodle Casserole

6 ounces uncooked wide egg noodles
1 teaspoon vegetable oil
1 onion, finely chopped
¾ cup thinly sliced celery
¾ cup thinly sliced carrot
1 can (about 15 ounces) salmon, drained, skin and bones discarded
1 can (10¾ ounces) condensed cream of celery soup, undiluted
1 cup (4 ounces) shredded Cheddar cheese
¾ cup frozen peas
½ cup sour cream
¼ cup milk
2 teaspoons dried dill weed
   Black pepper
   Fresh dill (optional)

1. Preheat oven to 350°F.

2. Cook noodles according to package directions; drain and return to saucepan.

3. Heat oil in large skillet over medium heat. Add onion, celery and carrot; cook and stir 5 minutes or until tender. Add onion mixture, salmon, soup, cheese, peas, sour cream, milk, dill weed and pepper to noodles; stir gently until blended. Pour into 2-quart baking dish.

4. Bake, covered, 25 minutes or until hot and bubbly. Garnish with fresh dill.

Makes 4 servings

tip

A member of the parsley family, dill weed is the dried soft feathery leaves of the dill plant. Its distinctive flavor can easily dominate a dish, so use it sparingly at first.

Sweet Potato Gratin

  3 pounds sweet potatoes (about 5 large)
½ cup (1 stick) butter, divided
¼ cup plus 2 tablespoons packed light brown sugar, divided
  2 eggs
⅔ cup orange juice
  2 teaspoons ground cinnamon, divided
½ teaspoon salt
¼ teaspoon ground nutmeg
⅓ cup all-purpose flour
¼ cup old-fashioned oats
⅓ cup chopped pecans or walnuts

1. Preheat oven to 350°F.

2. Bake sweet potatoes 1 hour or until tender. Let stand 5 minutes. Cut sweet potatoes lengthwise into halves. Scrape pulp from skins into large bowl.

3. Beat sweet potato pulp, ¼ cup butter and 2 tablespoons brown sugar with electric mixer at medium speed until butter is melted. Add eggs, orange juice, 1½ teaspoons cinnamon, salt and nutmeg; beat until smooth. Pour mixture into 6 (6-ounce) ovenproof ramekins or 1½-quart baking dish.

4. Combine flour, oats, remaining ¼ cup brown sugar and ½ teaspoon cinnamon in medium bowl. Cut in remaining ¼ cup butter with pastry blender or two knives until mixture resembles coarse crumbs. Stir in pecans. Sprinkle evenly over sweet potatoes.*

5. Bake 25 to 30 minutes or until heated through. For crispier topping, broil 5 inches from heat 2 to 3 minutes or until golden brown.   Makes 6 servings

At this point, Sweet Potato Gratin may be covered and refrigerated up to 1 day. Let stand at room temperature 1 hour before baking.

Corn Pudding

1 tablespoon butter
1 small onion, chopped
1 tablespoon all-purpose flour
2 cups half-and-half
1 cup milk
¼ cup quick-cooking grits or polenta
2 cups corn
4 eggs, lightly beaten
1 can (4 ounces) diced mild green chiles, drained
Salt and black pepper
¼ teaspoon hot pepper sauce

1. Preheat oven to 325°F. Grease 11×7-inch baking dish.

2. Melt butter in large saucepan over medium heat. Add onion; cook and stir 5 minutes or until tender and light golden. Stir in flour; cook until golden. Stir in half-and-half and milk; bring to a boil. Whisk in grits. Reduce heat to medium-low. Cook and stir 10 minutes or until mixture is thickened. Remove from heat. Stir in corn, eggs, chiles, salt, black pepper and hot pepper sauce. Pour into prepared baking dish.

3. Bake 1 hour or until knife inserted into center comes out clean.

Makes 8 servings

Broccoli Casserole

1 package (about 6 ounces) stuffing mix
1 can (10¾ ounces) condensed cream of mushroom soup, undiluted
1 package (10 ounces) frozen chopped broccoli, thawed
½ small onion, chopped
½ cup (2 ounces) shredded mozzarella cheese

1. Preheat oven to 350°F. Grease 2-quart casserole.

2. Prepare stuffing mix according to package directions. Add soup, broccoli and onion; mix well. Pour into prepared casserole. Sprinkle with cheese.

3. Bake 30 minutes or until heated through and cheese is melted.

Makes 4 servings

Corn Pudding

Spinach Casserole

3 tablespoons butter

1 tablespoon all-purpose flour

1 cup milk

2 eggs, separated

1 tablespoon chopped fresh parsley

   Salt and black pepper

1 cup (4 ounces) shredded Cheddar cheese

2 packages (14 ounces each) frozen chopped spinach, thawed and squeezed dry

1. Preheat oven to 350°F. Grease 2½-quart casserole.

2. Melt butter in medium saucepan over medium heat. Add flour; cook and stir 2 minutes. Gradually whisk in milk; cook until mixture thickens slightly. Beat egg yolks in small bowl; gradually stir into milk mixture. Season with parsley, salt and pepper. Add cheese, stirring constantly, until cheese melts. Transfer to medium bowl. Add spinach to cheese sauce; stir until well blended.

3. Beat egg whites in clean, dry bowl with electric mixer at high speed until stiff peaks form. Gently fold egg whites into spinach mixture. Spoon into prepared casserole.

4. Bake 40 minutes or until center is set. Makes 6 servings

Pasta & White Bean Casserole

1 tablespoon olive oil

½ cup chopped onion

2 cloves garlic, minced

2 cans (about 15 ounces each) cannellini beans, rinsed and drained

3 cups cooked small shell pasta

1 can (8 ounces) tomato sauce

1½ teaspoons Italian seasoning

   Salt and black pepper

1 cup (4 ounces) shredded Italian cheese blend

2 tablespoons finely chopped fresh Italian parsley

1. Preheat oven to 350°F. Lightly coat 2-quart casserole with nonstick cooking spray.

2. Heat oil in large skillet over medium heat. Add onion and garlic; cook and stir 4 minutes. Add beans, pasta, tomato sauce, Italian seasoning, salt and pepper; mix well. Transfer to prepared casserole; sprinkle with cheese and parsley.

3. Bake 20 minutes or until cheese is melted. Makes 6 servings

Spinach Casserole

Vegetable Gratin

2 tablespoons olive oil
3 small *or* 1 large zucchini, cut into ¼-inch slices
⅛ teaspoon salt, divided
⅛ teaspoon thyme, divided
⅛ teaspoon rosemary, divided
⅛ teaspoon freshly ground black pepper, divided
1 (6.5-ounce) package ALOUETTE® Savory Vegetable Spreadable Cheese
2 cups fresh broccoli florets
2 small yellow squash, sliced
1 small onion, sliced
1 cup crushed wheat crackers

• Preheat oven to 350°F. Place oil in medium-sized gratin or shallow baking dish.

• Layer zucchini in prepared dish.

• Sprinkle zucchini lightly with half each of salt, thyme, rosemary and pepper.

• Place 3 tablespoons Alouette® on top of zucchini.

• Layer with broccoli, yellow squash, onion, remaining seasonings and Alouette® until dish is filled.

• Sprinkle with cracker crumbs; cover with foil. Bake 20 minutes.

• Remove foil; bake another 20 minutes. Brown lightly under broiler 1 to 2 minutes. Serve hot or at room temperature.   Makes 6 to 8 servings

Note: This gratin is a delicious way to liven up vegetables! It's great with grilled chicken or steak.

Wild Rice Mushroom Stuffing

½ cup uncooked wild rice

4 ounces day-old French bread

½ cup (1 stick) butter

1 large onion, chopped

1 clove garlic, minced

3 cups sliced mushrooms

½ teaspoon rubbed sage

½ teaspoon dried thyme

Salt and black pepper

1 cup chicken broth

½ cup coarsely chopped pecans

Thyme sprigs (optional)

1. Prepare rice according to package directions; set aside.

2. Preheat broiler. Cut enough bread into ½-inch cubes to measure 4 cups. Spread in single layer on baking sheet. Broil 5 to 6 inches from heat 4 minutes or until lightly toasted, tossing after 2 minutes; set aside.

3. Preheat oven to 325°F.

4. Melt butter in large skillet over medium heat. Add onion and garlic; cook and stir 3 minutes. Add mushrooms; cook 3 minutes, stirring occasionally. Add rice, sage, dried thyme, salt and pepper; cook 2 minutes, stirring occasionally. Stir in broth. Add pecans and toasted bread cubes; toss lightly. Transfer to 1½-quart casserole.*

5. Bake, covered, 40 minutes or until heated through. Garnish with thyme sprigs.

Makes 6 to 8 servings

At this point, Wild Rice Mushroom Stuffing may be covered and refrigerated up to 8 hours before baking. Bake, covered, 50 minutes or until heated through.

Carrie's Sweet Potato Casserole

Brown Sugar Topping (recipe follows)
3 pounds sweet potatoes, cooked and peeled*
½ cup (1 stick) butter, softened
½ cup granulated sugar
½ cup evaporated milk
2 eggs
1 teaspoon vanilla
1 cup chopped pecans

You may substitute canned sweet potatoes.

1. Prepare Brown Sugar Topping.

2. Preheat oven to 350°F. Grease 8 (6-ounce) ovenproof ramekins.

3. Beat sweet potatoes and butter in large bowl with electric mixer at medium speed until light and fluffy. Add sugar, evaporated milk, eggs and vanilla, beating well after each addition. Spread evenly in prepared ramekins. Spoon Brown Sugar Topping over sweet potatoes; sprinkle with pecans.

4. Bake 20 to 25 minutes or until set.   Makes 8 servings

Brown Sugar Topping

1 cup packed brown sugar
½ cup all-purpose flour
⅓ cup butter, melted

Combine brown sugar, flour and butter in small bowl; mix well.

Makes about 1½ cups

Carrie's Sweet Potato Casserole

Herbed Cauliflower Casserole

5 cups cauliflower florets (about 1¼ pounds)
1 tablespoon butter, melted
1 small red bell pepper, cut into quarters
2 tablespoons water
3 large tomatoes, peeled, seeded and coarsely chopped
2 to 3 teaspoons chopped fresh tarragon
½ teaspoon chopped fresh parsley
⅓ cup (9 to 10) coarsely crushed saltine crackers

1. Preheat oven to 450°F.

2. Toss cauliflower with butter in large bowl; place cauliflower and bell pepper, cut sides down, in single layer in shallow baking pan. Add water to pan.

3. Bake 15 minutes. *Reduce oven temperature to 425°F.*

4. Bake 25 to 28 minutes or until cauliflower is tender and golden brown and bell pepper skin is blistered. Remove bell pepper pieces to plate and transfer cauliflower to 11×7-inch baking dish. *Reduce oven temperature to 400°F.*

5. Remove and discard skin from bell pepper. Place tomatoes and bell pepper in food processor; process until smooth. Add tarragon and parsley; process until blended. Pour tomato sauce over cauliflower.

6. Bake 10 minutes or until hot and bubbly. Sprinkle with cracker crumbs just before serving.   Makes 5 servings

Herbed Cauliflower Casserole

Toasted Coconut-Pecan Sweet Potato Casserole

2 cans (15 ounces each) sweet potatoes in heavy syrup, drained
½ cup (1 stick) butter, softened
¼ cup packed light brown sugar
1 egg
½ teaspoon vanilla
⅛ teaspoon salt
½ cup chopped pecans
¼ cup flaked sweetened coconut
2 tablespoons golden raisins

1. Preheat oven to 325°F. Spray 8-inch square baking dish with nonstick cooking spray.

2. Combine sweet potatoes, butter, brown sugar, egg, vanilla and salt in food processor or blender; process until smooth. Spoon into prepared dish. Sprinkle evenly with pecans, coconut and raisins.

3. Bake 22 minutes or until coconut is light golden brown.   Makes 4 servings

Orzo Casserole

2 tablespoons I CAN'T BELIEVE IT'S NOT BUTTER!® Spread
1 clove garlic, finely chopped
1½ cups uncooked orzo pasta
1 envelope LIPTON® RECIPE SECRETS® Onion or Onion Mushroom Soup Mix
3¼ cups water
6 ounces shiitake or white mushrooms, sliced
¼ cup chopped fresh parsley

In 3-quart heavy saucepan, melt I Can't Believe It's Not Butter!® Spread over medium heat and cook garlic with orzo, stirring constantly, 2½ minutes or until golden. Stir in soup mix blended with water. Bring to a boil over high heat. Reduce heat to low and simmer, covered, 10 minutes. Add mushrooms; *do not stir.* Simmer, covered, 10 minutes. Stir in parsley. Turn into serving bowl. (Liquid will not be totally absorbed.) Let stand 10 minutes or until liquid is absorbed.

Makes about 10 (½-cup) servings

Savory Orzo Casserole: Increase water to 4 cups and use Lipton® Recipe Secrets® Savory Herb with Garlic Soup Mix.

Toasted Coconut-Pecan Sweet Potato Casserole

Summer Squash Casserole

2 pounds small yellow summer squash, sliced

1 medium onion, sliced

¼ cup water

1 teaspoon salt

1 cup milk

2 large eggs, slightly beaten

3 tablespoons all-purpose flour

3 tablespoons CABOT® Salted Butter, melted, divided

½ teaspoon ground black pepper

2 cups grated CABOT® Sharp Cheddar (about 8 ounces), divided

¼ cup fresh bread crumbs

1. Preheat oven to 350°F. Butter 1½-quart baking dish or coat with nonstick cooking spray; set aside.

2. In saucepan, bring squash, onion, water and salt to a boil. Cover pan and simmer until squash is tender, about 20 minutes.

3. Drain squash and onion thoroughly, then mash. Add milk, eggs, flour, 1 tablespoon melted butter and pepper; mix well.

4. Reserve 3 tablespoons cheese; stir remaining cheese into squash mixture. Transfer squash mixture to prepared baking dish.

5. Bake for 30 minutes or until knife inserted into center comes out almost clean.

6. Meanwhile, toss bread crumbs with remaining 2 tablespoons melted butter. Sprinkle over casserole, then sprinkle with reserved cheese. Return to oven for 5 minutes or until crumbs are golden and cheese is melted.   Makes 8 servings

Wild Mushroom Baked Beans

1 package (3.5 ounces) fresh shiitake mushrooms, sliced

1 package (8 ounces) baby bella mushrooms, sliced

1 cup chopped onion

2 teaspoons minced garlic

2 tablespoons olive oil

2 tablespoons flour

1 can (15 ounces) pinto beans or 1½ cups cooked, dry-packaged pinto beans, rinsed and drained

1 can (15 ounces) Great Northern beans or 1½ cups cooked, dry-packaged Great Northern beans, rinsed and drained

1 can (15 ounces) red kidney beans or 1½ cups cooked, dry-packaged red kidney beans, rinsed and drained

1½ cups dry white wine or vegetable broth

¾ teaspoon dried thyme leaves

Finely chopped parsley

Sauté mushrooms, onion and garlic in oil in large skillet until tender, about 8 to 10 minutes. Stir in flour; cook 1 to 2 minutes.

Combine mushroom mixture, beans, wine and thyme in 2-quart casserole. Bake, uncovered, at 350°F 45 minutes. Sprinkle with parsley before serving.

Makes 12 (½-cup) servings

Prep Time: 15 to 20 minutes
Bake Time: 45 minutes

Substitutions: Any wild or domestic mushroom can be used in this recipe. Any canned or dry-packaged bean variety can be easily substituted for another.

Favorite recipe from **American Dry Bean Board**

Creamy Spinach Italiano

1 cup ricotta cheese
¾ cup half-and-half or milk
2 packages (10 ounces each) frozen chopped spinach, thawed and squeezed dry
1⅓ cups FRENCH'S® French Fried Onions, divided
½ cup chopped roasted red pepper
¼ cup chopped fresh basil
¼ cup grated Parmesan cheese
1 teaspoon garlic powder
¼ teaspoon salt

1. Preheat oven to 350°F. Whisk together ricotta cheese and half-and-half in large bowl until well combined. Stir in spinach, ⅔ *cup* French Fried Onions, red pepper, basil, Parmesan, garlic powder and salt. Pour mixture into greased deep-dish 9-inch pie plate.

2. Bake for 25 minutes or until heated through; stir. Sprinkle with remaining ⅔ *cup* onions. Bake for 5 minutes or until onions are golden.
Makes 4 servings

Prep Time: 10 minutes
Bake Time: 30 minutes

Festive Potato and Squash Casserole

3 pounds large baking potatoes, pierced with a fork
2 butternut squash (2½ pounds)
1 cup milk
1 teaspoon dried fines herbes
¼ teaspoon ground nutmeg
1¾ cups shredded JARLSBERG® cheese, divided
Salt and freshly ground black pepper to taste

Bake potatoes and squash in 350°F oven until tender, about 1¼ to 1½ hours. (Place foil under squash to prevent drips in oven.)

Scoop potato pulp into large bowl. Peel and seed squash. Using potato masher or electric beater, mash squash with potatoes, milk, fines herbes and nutmeg.

Stir 1¼ cups cheese into squash mixture; season with salt and pepper. Spoon mixture into shallow 2- or 2½-quart baking dish and sprinkle with remaining ½ cup cheese. Bake at 350°F for 30 to 40 minutes or until heated through and beginning to brown.
Makes 8 to 10 servings

Creamy Spinach Italiano

Baked Tomato Risotto

1 jar (28 ounces) pasta sauce
1 can (about 14 ounces) chicken broth
2 cups sliced zucchini
1 cup uncooked arborio rice
1 can (4 ounces) sliced mushrooms, drained
2 cups (8 ounces) shredded mozzarella cheese

1. Preheat oven to 350°F. Spray 3-quart casserole with nonstick cooking spray.

2. Combine pasta sauce, broth, zucchini, rice and mushrooms in prepared casserole.

3. Bake, covered, 30 minutes. Stir; bake, covered, 15 to 20 minutes or until rice is tender. Sprinkle evenly with cheese. Bake, uncovered, 5 minutes or until cheese is melted.

Makes 6 servings

Apricot and Walnut Brown Rice Stuffing

½ cup chopped onion
½ cup chopped celery
1 teaspoon margarine
3 cups cooked brown rice
⅔ cup coarsely chopped dried apricots
½ cup chicken broth
¼ cup coarsely chopped walnuts
¼ cup raisins, plumped
2 tablespoons snipped parsley
½ teaspoon dried thyme leaves
¼ teaspoon salt
¼ teaspoon rubbed sage
¼ teaspoon ground black pepper

Cook onion and celery in margarine in large skillet over medium-high heat until tender-crisp. Add rice, apricots, broth, walnuts, raisins, parsley, thyme, salt, sage and pepper; transfer to 2-quart baking dish. Bake in covered baking dish at 375°F for 15 to 20 minutes. (Stuffing may be baked inside poultry.)   *Makes 6 servings*

Tip: To plump raisins, cover with 1 cup boiling water. Let stand 1 to 2 minutes; drain.

Favorite recipe from **USA Rice**

Baked Tomato Risotto

Broccoli & Cheese Casserole

1 can (10¾ ounces) CAMPBELL'S® Condensed Cream of Mushroom Soup
(Regular or 98% Fat Free)

½ cup milk

2 teaspoons yellow mustard

1 bag (16 ounces) frozen broccoli florets, thawed

1 cup shredded Cheddar cheese (4 ounces)

⅓ cup dry bread crumbs

2 teaspoons butter, melted

1. Stir the soup, milk, mustard, broccoli and cheese in a 1½-quart casserole.

2. Stir the bread crumbs and butter in a small bowl. Sprinkle the crumb mixture over the broccoli mixture.

3. Bake at 350°F. for 30 minutes or until the mixture is hot and bubbling.

Makes 6 servings

Prep Time: 10 minutes
Bake Time: 30 minutes
Total Time: 40 minutes

Rice Is Nice: Add 2 cups cooked white rice to the broccoli mixture before baking.
Cheese Change-Up: Substitute mozzarella cheese for the Cheddar.

Potato 'n' Onion Bake

1 pound all-purpose or baking potatoes, thinly sliced

2 medium onions, thinly sliced

2 tablespoons olive oil

½ teaspoon salt

½ teaspoon ground black pepper

2 cups RAGÚ® Chunky Pasta Sauce

3 tablespoons grated Parmesan cheese

1. Preheat oven to 400°F.

2. In 2-quart baking dish, layer ½ of the potatoes, onions, olive oil, salt and pepper; repeat layers. Bake, covered, 20 minutes or until potatoes are tender. Remove cover; pour Pasta Sauce over potato mixture; sprinkle with Parmesan cheese. Bake an additional 10 minutes or until heated through.

Makes 4 servings

Broccoli & Cheese Casserole

Apple & Carrot Casserole

6 large carrots, sliced

4 large apples, peeled, cored and sliced

¼ cup plus 1 tablespoon all-purpose flour

1 tablespoon packed brown sugar

½ teaspoon ground nutmeg

1 tablespoon butter

½ cup orange juice

½ teaspoon salt

1. Preheat oven to 350°F.

2. Cook carrots in boiling water in large saucepan 5 minutes; drain. Layer carrots and apples in 2-quart casserole.

3. Combine flour, brown sugar and nutmeg in small bowl; sprinkle over top. Dot with butter; pour orange juice over casserole. Sprinkle with salt.

4. Bake 30 minutes or until carrots are tender. Makes 6 servings

Autumn Veg•All® Barley Bake

2 tablespoons vegetable oil

2 cloves garlic, diced

2 cups chopped celery

1 can (15 ounces) VEG•ALL® Original Mixed Vegetables, drained

½ teaspoon salt

½ teaspoon pepper

¼ teaspoon thyme

¼ teaspoon marjoram

¾ cup dried sweetened cranberries

1 cup quick cooking barley, cooked according to package directions

¼ cup Allens Chicken Broth

Preheat oven to 350°F. In large frying pan, heat oil. Sauté garlic and celery until tender; remove from heat.

Stir in Veg•All, salt, pepper, thyme, marjoram, cranberries, barley and chicken broth.

Pour into 3-quart greased casserole dish.

Bake, covered, 20 to 25 minutes; serve hot. Makes 8 servings

Apple & Carrot Casserole

Cheesy Green Bean Casserole

¾ cup milk

2 teaspoons all-purpose flour

1 teaspoon dried minced onion

½ teaspoon black pepper

1 package (16 ounces) frozen cut green beans, thawed

1 cup (4 ounces) shredded Cheddar cheese, divided

¼ cup seasoned dry bread crumbs

1. Preheat oven to 350°F.

2. Whisk milk, flour, onion and pepper in medium bowl until well blended. Pour into 1½-quart baking dish. Stir in green beans and ½ cup cheese.

3. Bake 25 minutes. Sprinkle with remaining ½ cup cheese and bread crumbs. Bake 5 minutes or until cheese is melted.   Makes 6 servings

Baked Corn Casserole

1 can (10¾ ounces) CAMPBELL'S® Condensed Cream of Chicken Soup
    (Regular or 98% Fat Free)

½ cup milk

2 eggs

1 can (about 16 ounces) whole kernel corn, drained

1 package (about 8 ounces) corn muffin mix

¼ cup grated Parmesan cheese

1 can (2.8 ounces) French fried onions (about 1⅓ cups)

1. Beat the soup, milk and eggs in a medium bowl with a fork or whisk. Stir in the corn, corn muffin mix, cheese and ⅔ cup onions. Pour the soup mixture into a 1½-quart casserole.

2. Bake at 350°F. for 30 minutes or until the mixture is hot.

3. Top with the remaining onions. Bake for 5 minutes or until the onions are golden brown.   Makes 6 servings

Prep Time: 10 minutes
Bake Time: 35 minutes
Total Time: 45 minutes

Cheesy Green Bean Casserole

Grated Potato and Blue Cheese Casserole

1 tablespoon butter

1½ cups finely chopped red onions

1 package (8 ounces) Neufchâtel cheese, softened

¼ to ⅓ cup crumbled blue cheese

¾ cup whipping cream

1 tablespoon minced fresh thyme *or* 1 teaspoon dried thyme

½ teaspoon salt

2 pounds baking potatoes (about 4 medium)

Fresh thyme sprigs and red pearl onion wedges (optional)

1. Preheat oven to 350°F. Grease 11×7-inch baking dish.

2. Melt butter in large skillet over medium heat. Add onions; cook and stir 5 minutes or until onions are translucent. Remove from heat.

3. Beat Neufchâtel cheese in large bowl with electric mixer at medium speed until fluffy. Add blue cheese; beat until blended. Beat in cream, minced thyme and salt at low speed until mixture is smooth. (There will be some small lumps.) Add onions; beat until blended.

4. Peel potatoes. Grate 1 potato; fold into cheese mixture. Repeat with remaining potatoes. Pour mixture into prepared baking dish.

5. Bake, covered, 45 minutes. Bake, uncovered, 15 to 20 minutes or until crisp around edges.

6. Preheat broiler. Broil 6 inches from heat 3 to 5 minutes or until top is golden brown. Let stand 5 minutes before serving. Garnish with thyme sprigs and onion wedges.

Makes 6 servings

Grated Potato and Blue Cheese Casserole

Baked Risotto with Asparagus, Spinach & Parmesan

1 tablespoon olive oil
1 cup finely chopped onion
1 cup uncooked arborio rice
8 cups (8 to 10 ounces) packed torn stemmed spinach
2 cups vegetable broth
¼ teaspoon salt
¼ teaspoon ground nutmeg
½ cup grated Parmesan cheese, divided
1½ cups sliced asparagus

1. Preheat oven to 400°F. Spray 13×9-inch baking dish with nonstick cooking spray.

2. Heat oil in large skillet over medium-high heat. Add onion; cook and stir 4 minutes or until tender. Add rice; stir to coat with oil.

3. Stir in spinach, a handful at a time, adding more as it wilts. Reduce heat to medium. Add broth, salt and nutmeg; simmer 7 minutes. Stir in ¼ cup cheese. Transfer to prepared baking dish.

4. Bake, covered, 15 minutes. Stir in asparagus; sprinkle with remaining ¼ cup cheese. Bake, covered, 15 minutes or until liquid is absorbed.

Makes 10 to 12 servings

Baked Risotto with Asparagus, Spinach & Parmesan

Wild Rice Casserole

1 cup wild rice, soaked overnight, drained
1 large onion, chopped
1 cup (4 ounces) shredded Cheddar cheese
1 cup chopped mushrooms
1 cup chopped black olives
1 cup drained chopped tomatoes
1 cup tomato juice
⅓ cup vegetable oil
   Salt and black pepper

1. Preheat oven to 350°F.

2. Combine rice, onion, cheese, mushrooms, olives, tomatoes, tomato juice and oil in large bowl. Season with salt and pepper. Transfer rice mixture to 2½- to 3-quart casserole.

3. Bake, covered, 1 hour and 30 minutes or until rice is tender.   Makes 6 servings

Southwest Spaghetti Squash

1 spaghetti squash (about 3 pounds)
1 can (about 14 ounces) Mexican-style diced tomatoes
1 can (about 14 ounces) black beans, rinsed and drained
¾ cup (3 ounces) shredded Monterey Jack cheese, divided
¼ cup finely chopped fresh cilantro
1 teaspoon ground cumin
¼ teaspoon garlic salt
¼ teaspoon black pepper

1. Preheat oven to 350°F. Spray baking sheet and 1½-quart baking dish with nonstick cooking spray.

2. Cut squash in half lengthwise. Remove and discard seeds. Place squash, cut side down, on prepared baking sheet.

3. Bake 45 minutes or just until tender. Shred squash with fork; place in large bowl. Add tomatoes, beans, ½ cup cheese, cilantro, cumin, garlic salt and pepper; toss well. Spoon mixture into prepared baking dish. Sprinkle with remaining ¼ cup cheese.

4. Bake 30 to 35 minutes or until heated through.   Makes 4 servings

Wild Rice Casserole

Acorn Squash with Corn Bread Stuffing

1 acorn squash (about 2 pounds)
¼ cup (½ stick) butter, divided
2 cups chopped mushrooms
1 medium onion, chopped
1 stalk celery, chopped
¾ cup seasoned corn bread stuffing mix
Salt and black pepper
2 tablespoons packed brown sugar

1. Cut squash into quarters; remove and discard seeds. Place squash, skin side up, in microwavable dish; add ½ inch water. Cover loosely with plastic wrap; microwave on HIGH 8 to 10 minutes or until tender. Drain well.

2. Preheat oven to 375°F. Melt 2 tablespoons butter in large saucepan over medium heat. Add mushrooms, onion and celery; cook and stir 7 to 10 minutes or until tender. Remove from heat. Stir in stuffing mix, salt and pepper.

3. Place squash in 2-quart baking dish, cut side up. Top each quarter with remaining 2 tablespoons butter and brown sugar. Pack stuffing evenly onto each quarter.

4. Bake 25 to 30 minutes or until stuffing is golden brown.   Makes 4 servings

Broccoli-Rice Casserole

1 tablespoon olive oil
½ cup *each* chopped onion and chopped celery
⅓ cup chopped red bell pepper
1 can (10¾ ounces) condensed broccoli and cheese soup, undiluted
¼ cup sour cream
2 cups cooked rice
1 package (10 ounces) frozen chopped broccoli, thawed and drained
1 tomato, cut into ¼-inch-thick slices

1. Preheat oven to 350°F. Spray 1½-quart baking dish with nonstick cooking spray.

2. Heat oil in large skillet over medium heat. Add onion, celery and bell pepper; cook and stir until tender. Stir in soup and sour cream. Layer rice and broccoli in prepared baking dish. Top evenly with soup mixture.

3. Bake, covered, 20 minutes. Top with tomato slices. Bake, uncovered, 10 minutes.
Makes 6 servings

Acorn Squash with Corn Bread Stuffing

Fresh Vegetable Casserole

8 small new potatoes

8 baby carrots

1 head cauliflower, broken into florets

4 stalks asparagus, cut into 1-inch pieces

3 tablespoons butter

3 tablespoons all-purpose flour

2 cups milk

　Salt and black pepper

¾ cup (3 ounces) shredded Cheddar cheese

　Chopped fresh cilantro or parsley

1. Preheat oven to 350°F. Grease 2-quart casserole.

2. Steam potatoes, carrots, cauliflower and asparagus until crisp-tender. Arrange vegetables in prepared casserole.

3. Melt butter in medium saucepan over medium heat. Stir in flour until smooth; gradually whisk in milk. Bring to a boil. Cook and stir 2 minutes or until thick and bubbly. Season with salt and pepper. Add cheese, stirring until melted. Pour sauce over vegetables and sprinkle with cilantro.

4. Bake 15 minutes or until heated through.　　　　Makes 4 to 6 servings

Spinach-Cheese Pasta Casserole

8 ounces uncooked shell pasta

2 eggs

1 cup ricotta cheese

1 package (10 ounces) frozen chopped spinach, thawed and squeezed dry

1 jar (26 ounces) marinara sauce

1 teaspoon salt

1 cup (4 ounces) shredded mozzarella cheese

¼ cup grated Parmesan cheese

1. Preheat oven to 350°F. Spray 1½-quart casserole with nonstick cooking spray.

2. Cook pasta according to package directions; drain.

3. Whisk eggs in large bowl until blended. Add ricotta cheese and spinach to eggs; stir until blended. Stir in pasta, marinara sauce and salt until pasta is well coated. Pour into prepared casserole. Sprinkle mozzarella and Parmesan cheeses evenly over casserole.

4. Bake, covered, 30 minutes. Bake, uncovered, 15 minutes or until hot and bubbly.

Makes 6 to 8 servings

Barley Vegetable Casserole

2¼ cups vegetable broth, divided

⅔ cup uncooked barley (not quick-cooking)

4 cups frozen mixed vegetables (broccoli, cauliflower, carrots and onions)

½ teaspoon salt

½ teaspoon garlic powder

¼ teaspoon black pepper

1 tablespoon butter

1. Preheat oven to 350°F. Spray 1-quart casserole with nonstick cooking spray.

2. Place ¼ cup broth and barley in medium nonstick skillet; cook over medium heat 3 minutes or until lightly browned, stirring frequently. Transfer to prepared casserole. Add vegetables, salt, garlic powder, pepper and remaining 2 cups broth to casserole; mix well.

3. Bake, covered, 50 minutes or until barley is tender and most liquid is absorbed, stirring several times during baking. Stir in butter. Let stand 5 minutes before serving.

Makes 4 servings

Spinach-Cheese Pasta Casserole

Eggplant Parmesan

½ cup olive or vegetable oil
1 medium eggplant (about 1½ pounds), peeled, sliced
1 carton (15 ounces) ricotta cheese
1 can (15 ounces) CONTADINA® Tomato Sauce with Italian Herbs
1 clove garlic, minced
½ teaspoon dried oregano leaves, crushed
½ cup CONTADINA Seasoned Bread Crumbs
2 tablespoons grated Parmesan cheese

1. Heat oil in large skillet. Add eggplant; cook for 2 to 3 minutes on each side or until tender. Remove from oil with slotted spoon. Drain on paper towels.

2. Place half of eggplant slices in greased 12×7½-inch baking dish. Spoon half of ricotta cheese over eggplant.

3. Combine tomato sauce, garlic and oregano in small bowl. Pour half of tomato sauce mixture over ricotta cheese.

4. Combine bread crumbs and Parmesan cheese in separate small bowl; sprinkle half over top of sauce mixture. Repeat layers.

5. Bake in preheated 350°F oven for 30 minutes or until sauce is bubbly.

Makes 6 servings

Prep Time: 20 minutes
Bake Time: 30 minutes

Green Beans with Blue Cheese and Roasted Peppers

1 package (20 ounces) frozen cut green beans
3 ounces jarred roasted red pepper strips, drained and slivered
⅛ teaspoon salt
⅛ teaspoon white pepper
4 ounces cream cheese
½ cup milk
¾ cup (3 ounces) crumbled blue cheese
½ cup Italian-seasoned dry bread crumbs
1 tablespoon butter, melted

1. Preheat oven to 350°F. Spray 2-quart casserole with nonstick cooking spray.

2. Combine green beans, red pepper strips, salt and white pepper in prepared casserole.

3. Place cream cheese and milk in small saucepan; heat over low heat, stirring until melted. Add blue cheese; stir just until combined. Pour cheese mixture over green bean mixture; stir until green beans are coated. Combine bread crumbs and butter in small bowl; sprinkle evenly over casserole.

4. Bake 20 minutes or until hot and bubbly.   Makes 4 servings

White Bean and Ripe Olive Gratin

     2 tablespoons olive oil
     1 cup thinly sliced celery
    ½ cup thinly sliced red onion
     1 teaspoon minced garlic
     2 cups seeded, diced Roma tomatoes
     2 cups diced zucchini (¼-inch)
     2 cups sliced California Ripe Olives
    ¼ cup chopped fresh sage
     2 (15-ounce) cans white beans, rinsed
     1 cup fresh bread crumbs
    ¼ cup chopped parsley
     2 tablespoons olive oil
     1 teaspoon minced garlic
     1 teaspoon lemon zest

Preheat oven to 350°F. Heat 2 tablespoons olive oil in heavy pot. Add celery, onion and 1 teaspoon garlic. Sauté over medium-high heat for 3 minutes. Add tomatoes and zucchini; simmer for 5 minutes. Remove from heat. Add olives and sage. Purée about ¼ of the beans and add all beans to tomato mixture. Mix well and adjust seasoning with salt and pepper. Transfer to a buttered 2-quart shallow baking dish. Combine bread crumbs, parsley, 2 tablespoons olive oil, 1 teaspoon garlic and lemon zest in small bowl. Mix well and sprinkle evenly over casserole. Bake at 350°F until bubbly and golden, about 45 minutes. Let rest 5 or 10 minutes before serving.

Makes 8 servings

Favorite recipe from **California Olive Industry**

Zucchini with Feta Casserole

4 medium zucchini

1 tablespoon butter

2 eggs, beaten

½ cup grated Parmesan cheese

⅓ cup crumbled feta cheese

2 tablespoons chopped fresh parsley

1 tablespoon all-purpose flour

2 teaspoons chopped fresh marjoram

   Dash hot pepper sauce

   Salt and black pepper

1. Preheat oven to 375°F. Grease 2-quart casserole.

2. Grate zucchini; drain in colander. Melt butter in medium skillet over medium heat. Add zucchini; cook and stir until slightly browned. Remove from heat. Add eggs, cheeses, parsley, flour, marjoram, hot pepper sauce, salt and black pepper to skillet; mix well. Pour into prepared casserole.

3. Bake 35 minutes or until hot and bubbly.

Makes 4 servings

Scalloped Potatoes with Gorgonzola

1 (14½-ounce) can chicken broth

1½ cups whipping cream

4 teaspoons minced garlic

1½ teaspoons dried sage leaves

1 cup BELGIOIOSO® Gorgonzola Cheese

2¼ pounds russet potatoes, peeled, halved and thinly sliced

   Salt and pepper to taste

Preheat oven to 375°F. In medium heavy saucepan, simmer chicken broth, whipping cream, garlic and sage 5 minutes or until slightly thickened. Add BelGioioso Gorgonzola Cheese and stir until melted. Remove from heat.

Place potatoes in large bowl and season with salt and pepper. Arrange half of potatoes in 13×9×2-inch glass baking dish. Pour half of cream mixture over top of potatoes. Repeat layers with remaining potatoes and cream mixture. Bake until potatoes are tender, about 1¼ hours. Let stand 15 minutes before serving.

Makes 8 servings

Zucchini with Feta Casserole

Party Potatoes Italiano

Nonstick cooking spray
1 can (14.5 ounces) Italian-style diced tomatoes
1 cup panko (Japanese bread crumbs)
1 package (30 ounces) frozen hash brown potatoes, thawed
1½ cups sour cream
1¼ cups (3.75 ounces) BUITONI® Refrigerated Freshly Shredded Parmesan Cheese
1 can (10.75 ounces) reduced-fat cream of chicken soup
⅔ cup (5 fluid-ounce can) NESTLÉ® CARNATION® Evaporated Milk
2 tablespoons olive oil
1 teaspoon onion powder
1 teaspoon Italian herb seasoning
½ teaspoon salt
½ teaspoon freshly ground black pepper
2 tablespoons chopped fresh basil or parsley

PREHEAT oven to 350°F. Spray 13×9-inch baking dish with nonstick cooking spray.

PLACE tomatoes in a strainer set over a bowl. Let juice drain for 15 minutes; reserve juice. Toss drained tomatoes with bread crumbs in medium bowl; set aside for later use.

COMBINE hash browns, sour cream, cheese, soup, evaporated milk, oil, onion powder, Italian seasoning, salt, pepper and reserved juice from tomatoes in large bowl. Spread potato mixture evenly into prepared dish. Sprinkle tomato mixture over top.

BAKE for 1 hour or until bubbly at the edges. Sprinkle with fresh basil or parsley before serving.

Makes 12 servings

Prep Time: 20 minutes
Baking Time: 1 hour

Acknowledgments

The publisher would like to thank the companies and organizations listed below for the use of their recipes and photographs in this publication.

Alouette® Spreadable Cheese,
Alouette® Baby Brie®,
Alouette® Crème Spreadable,
Chavrie®, Saladena®

BelGioioso® Cheese Inc.

Bob Evans®

Cabot® Creamery Cooperative

California Olive Committee

Campbell Soup Company

Colorado Potato Administrative Committee

Cream of Wheat® Cereal

Del Monte Foods

Dole Food Company, Inc.

Florida Department of Agriculture and
Consumer Services,
Bureau of Seafood and Aquaculture

The Golden Grain Company®

Hormel Foods, LLC

Kraft Foods Global, Inc.

Minnesota Cultivated Wild Rice Council

National Pork Board

Nestlé USA

jarlsbergusa.com

North Dakota Beef Commission

North Dakota Wheat Commission

Reckitt Benckiser LLC.

Riviana Foods Inc.

Sargento® Foods Inc.

Tyson Foods, Inc.

Unilever

USA Rice Federation®

US Dry Bean Council

Veg•All®

Watkins Incorporated

Wisconsin Milk Marketing Board

Index

Index

Index

Metric Conversion Chart

VOLUME MEASUREMENTS (dry)

⅛ teaspoon = 0.5 mL
¼ teaspoon = 1 mL
½ teaspoon = 2 mL
¾ teaspoon = 4 mL
1 teaspoon = 5 mL
1 tablespoon = 15 mL
2 tablespoons = 30 mL
¼ cup = 60 mL
⅓ cup = 75 mL
½ cup = 125 mL
⅔ cup = 150 mL
¾ cup = 175 mL
1 cup = 250 mL
2 cups = 1 pint = 500 mL
3 cups = 750 mL
4 cups = 1 quart = 1 L

VOLUME MEASUREMENTS (fluid)

1 fluid ounce (2 tablespoons) = 30 mL
4 fluid ounces (½ cup) = 125 mL
8 fluid ounces (1 cup) = 250 mL
12 fluid ounces (1½ cups) = 375 mL
16 fluid ounces (2 cups) = 500 mL

WEIGHTS (mass)

½ ounce = 15 g
1 ounce = 30 g
3 ounces = 90 g
4 ounces = 120 g
8 ounces = 225 g
10 ounces = 285 g
12 ounces = 360 g
16 ounces = 1 pound = 450 g

DIMENSIONS

1/16 inch = 2 mm
⅛ inch = 3 mm
¼ inch = 6 mm
½ inch = 1.5 cm
¾ inch = 2 cm
1 inch = 2.5 cm

OVEN TEMPERATURES

250°F = 120°C
275°F = 140°C
300°F = 150°C
325°F = 160°C
350°F = 180°C
375°F = 190°C
400°F = 200°C
425°F = 220°C
450°F = 230°C

BAKING PAN SIZES

Utensil	Size in Inches/Quarts	Metric Volume	Size in Centimeters
Baking or Cake Pan (square or rectangular)	8×8×2	2 L	20×20×5
	9×9×2	2.5 L	23×23×5
	12×8×2	3 L	30×20×5
	13×9×2	3.5 L	33×23×5
Loaf Pan	8×4×3	1.5 L	20×10×7
	9×5×3	2 L	23×13×7
Round Layer Cake Pan	8×1½	1.2 L	20×4
	9×1½	1.5 L	23×4
Pie Plate	8×1¼	750 mL	20×3
	9×1¼	1 L	23×3
Baking Dish or Casserole	1 quart	1 L	—
	1½ quart	1.5 L	—
	2 quart	2 L	—